W9-BRC-601

Better Homes and Gardens®

YOUR FURNITURE

First Edition. Second Printing, 1984.
Library of Congress Catalog Card Number: 82-81726
ISBN: 0-696-02170-6

BETTER HOMES AND GARDENS® BOOKS

Editor: Gerald M. Knox
Art Director: Ernest Shelton
Managing Editor: David A. Kirchner

Associate Art Directors: Linda Ford Vermie, Neoma Alt West, Randall Yontz
Copy and Production Editors: Marsha Jahns, Mary Helen Schiltz, Carl Voss, David A. Walsh
Assistant Art Directors: Harijs Priekulis, Tom Wegner
Senior Graphic Designers: Alisann Dixon, Lynda Haupert, Lyne Neymeyer
Graphic Designers: Mike Burns, Mike Eagleton, Deb Miner, Stan Sams, D. Greg Thompson, Darla Whipple, Paul Zimmerman

Vice President, Editorial Director: Doris Eby
Group Editorial Services Director: Duane L. Gregg

General Manager: Fred Stines
Director of Publishing: Robert B. Nelson
Vice President, Director of Retail Marketing: Jamie Martin
Vice President, Director of Direct Marketing: Arthur Heydendael

All About Your House: Your Furniture

Project Editor: James A. Hufnagel
Associate Editor: Willa Rosenblatt Speiser
Assistant Editor: Leonore A. Levy
Copy and Production Editor: David A. Walsh
Building and Remodeling Editor: Joan McCloskey
Furnishings and Design Editor: Shirley Van Zante
Garden Editor: Douglas A. Jimerson
Money Management and Features Editor: Margaret Daly

Art Director: Linda Ford Vermie
Graphic Designer: Darla Whipple

Contributing Editor: Karol Brookhouser
Contributing Senior Writer: Paul Kitzke
Contributors: Mary Bryson, Denise L. Caringer, Pamela Wilson Cullison, Anne Elizabeth Powell

Special thanks to William N. Hopkins, Bill Hopkins, Jr., Babs Klein, and Don Wipperman for their valuable contributions to this book.

INTRODUCTION

Of all a home's contents, its furnishings probably say the most about the family that lives there. The colors you choose; the textures you favor; whether you like things that are old, new, or a combination of both; even the way you arrange your furniture—all are very personal statements of your family's tastes and life-style.

Neither a textbook about period furniture styles nor a portfolio of the latest in home fashion, *Your Furniture* is a book about *your* furniture. It focuses on using the pieces you now have, as well as on choosing new ones. You'll learn how to mix and match with confidence, how to create workable room arrangements, how to select good pieces, and how to refurbish and care for everything from wicker to wood to upholstery.

Along with practical advice that can guide you through all stages of furnishing or refurnishing a home, *Your Furniture* includes more than 100 color photographs of room settings and individual pieces. Styles range from elegant traditional to striking contemporary to unexpected eclectic. Among these styles, we hope you'll find some favorites that can inspire you to look at your own rooms in different ways.

By now you may already be familiar with the ALL ABOUT YOUR HOUSE Library. From doorknobs to dormers, gardens to guest rooms, this wide-ranging series of books from the editors at Better Homes and Gardens® covers almost every aspect of improving and decorating a modern-day home—*your* home.

YOUR FURNITURE

CONTENTS

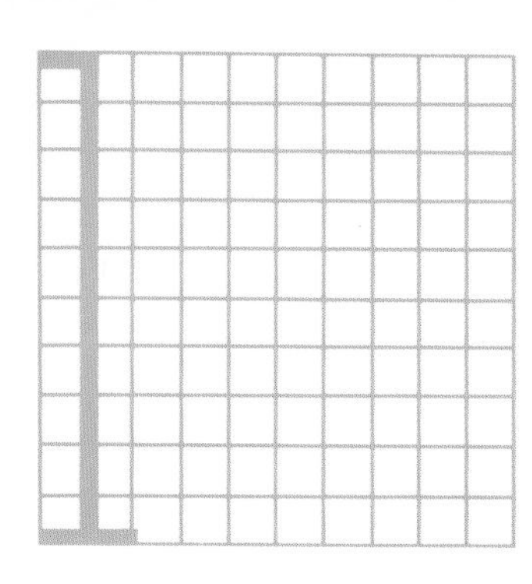

BEGINNING QUESTIONS

Faced with an empty room, no two people will furnish it the same way. One person's comfortable place to sit may be a well-upholstered wing chair; another's may be a modular unit with matching ottoman. Because choosing and arranging furniture have everything to do with individual preference, lifestyle, and budget, this opening chapter focuses on you and your priorities. Once you've thought about the role furniture plays in your life, you'll be ready to read more about furniture itself—how to choose and use it, how to recycle and maintain it, and more—in the chapters that follow.

WHAT ARE YOUR NEEDS?

Do budget and space restrictions or a strong preference for a special period limit your furniture-shopping expeditions? Or do you like lots of different things, and buy whatever catches your eye? No matter how narrow or diverse your preferences, the furniture that's right for you is waiting to be found. That's why it's important to sit down and list your needs *before* shopping for new furniture.

This kind of list-making is not only necessary but also fun. Kick off your shoes, sit back, and daydream. Have you always wanted to lounge on a chaise on a cold winter day? Consider replacing your present sofa and chairs with a chaise longue or two. Is there a writer lurking inside you? Then put "desk space" high on your list. Want to be more comfortable on your porch or deck? Today's attractive, versatile outdoor furnishings can help.

As you make your room-by-room checklist, refer especially to Chapter 3—"New Furniture Options"; Chapter 5—"Shopping Sense"; and Chapter 7—"Outdoor Furniture."

To get you started, note how the living room pictured *at right* meets diverse requirements—a modest budget coupled with high-style taste and a need for guest sleeping space. The result: a dramatic room where elegance and low cost go hand-in-hand. The chaises set an indulgent mood, but they're actually budget-pleasing foam pieces that fold out into beds. The pull-up armchair has the sleek silhouette of a Bauhaus original, but it's merely a moderately priced outdoor piece. In the background, two old tables and a pair of Windsor-like chairs add antique touches to the otherwise modern setting.

CENTER COLLEGE OF DESIGN

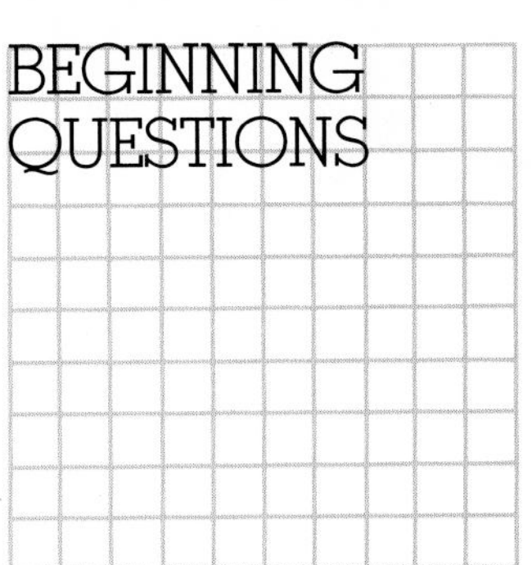

WHAT ARE YOUR PRIORITIES?

Once you know what you need, set priorities. Analyze what you want most—and what you can do without for a while. Can you completely furnish your entire home at once, or will you focus on one or two rooms? Do you need a formal dining room, or would the space and money be better devoted to a family room? Can you do without a guest room in order to have the home office you've always wanted? Once you have your priorities in order, it's easier to make specific furnishings choices.

When it comes to setting furnishings priorities, there's no one right answer. Let your budget and personality guide you.

They may dictate that you furnish your entire home in one fell swoop with modestly priced pieces, or decorate one room each year with more expensive items. Or, if you believe fine furniture is worth a wait, buy one piece at a time—a beautifully upholstered sofa, a leather chair, a special rug—over several years.

No matter which approach you take, you'll find that well-designed furnishings come in all price ranges.

More for less

If you won't feel settled until all the rooms in your home are more or less properly furnished, the "more-for-less" approach may be best for you. If you have an eye for value and simple lines, you'll find low- to medium-priced items that will let you complete your furnishings plan without wreaking havoc with family finances.

Consider starting your room with one or two major pieces (like the two chaises in the room shown on the preceding two pages). Next, look for other furnishings to fill in the gaps—a chair for auxiliary seating, a couple of modestly priced lamps, and perhaps a secondhand table and chair for dining and desk work.

For a coffee table that's easy on your finances, look for quick-assembly pieces you take home in a box and put together yourself. (For more about easy-to-assemble pieces, see pages 40 and 41.) Or simply top a basket, a homemade wooden cube, or some other found-object base with a piece of plate glass.

Finally, seek out a few low-cost finishing touches: a budget-priced area rug (sisal or rush matting, a woven rag rug, or a carpet remnant with bound edges); a framed poster, a piece of stretched fabric, or your children's watercolors; and a few plants.

Building up

Selecting one choice piece of furniture at a time not only will help you stay within your budget, it also will enable your decorating scheme to evolve surely as well as slowly.

Buying one stellar item doesn't mean living with a bare room until your next purchase. As you can see from the warm and inviting breakfast spot pictured *at left,* one piece—in this case the beautifully crafted Welsh dresser—can set the tone for an entire room and blend easily with less-costly items.

Here, two inexpensive ladder-back chairs from an unfinished-furniture store were painted black and teamed with a worn, secondhand game table from a garage sale. (For advice about selecting unfinished furniture, see page 81; to learn about recycling furniture, see Chapter 9.)

Since choice accessories must wait until later, the gaps have been filled with interesting, low-cost accents. Baskets hang from the ceiling beams, and plants and flowering tree branches are displayed in other found-object containers.

The Welsh dresser itself displays a mix of family heirlooms and newfound bargains. Among the bargains: low-cost blue-and-white plates for color and pattern, and modestly priced stoneware pitchers for homespun charm.

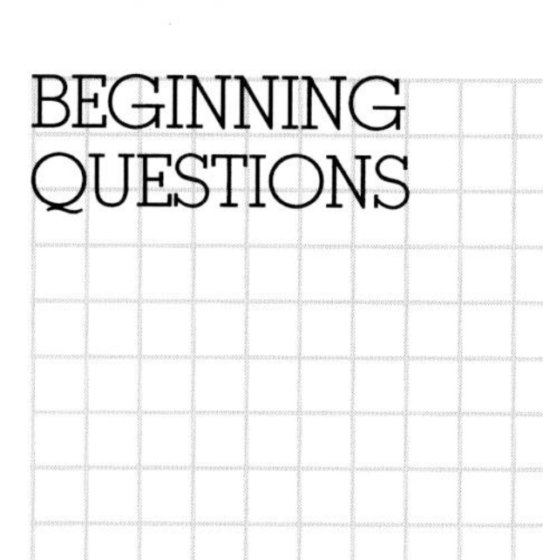

HOW MUCH CAN YOU SPEND?

No matter how clear-cut your priorities are and no matter how well-defined your taste, the amount of money you have available is a key factor in any furniture-purchasing decisions you make. Establish a realistic budget—and reinforce your resolve to stick to it. Good design doesn't have to wear an expensive price tag, and there are many ways to get the look you want at the price you can afford.

As you think about your budget, the timetable you select will take on added meaning. Decide to furnish and decorate your living room and dining room in the next couple of months, and your budget will tell you one thing; opt to do the job over the next year or two, and the financial picture will be entirely different.

You'll get the most for your money if you're aware of furnishings options and know how to judge the quality of both new and used furniture. For more about these all-important aspects of buymanship, see Chapter 5 for a general overview. Then turn to Chapter 6—"Antiques, Reproductions, Adaptations, and Handcrafted Furniture"—and Chapter 9—"Recycling Furniture." If you're interested in building your own economical, long-lasting furniture, see Chapter 8—"Furniture You Can Make Yourself."

Furnishing step by step

For many people, installment decorating is the most sensible approach. By doing one room at a time in manageable stages, you can stretch your expenses out over months or years. This gives you time to make choices you can live with happily for years.

For example, if you're in a hurry to furnish a dining room, you may quickly opt for a matched group of pieces (a table, chairs, a china cabinet) from a showroom floor. Buying everything now may mean settling for lower quality than you really want.

Instead, you might start with one terrific item—say, a pine country table that seats eight—and scout around for some interesting secondhand chairs to go with it. Then fill in the gaps with budget-pleasing accessories—a wall-hung shelf to double as display and serving space, a tall plant to soften a corner, and a framed poster or a piece of stretched fabric. Now sit back, let your budget recuperate, and live with your room for a while. If you once assumed you needed a china cabinet, you may now decide you don't—and save yourself several hundred dollars. Or in the interim you may have found an antique cupboard or armoire that provides just the right finishing touch.

Case history

The inviting solarium pictured *at left* testifies to the advantages of decorating in stages. By letting the room evolve at a moderate pace, the owners achieved a personable, nonchalant mix of compatible items far more interesting than a set of perfectly matched furnishings.

After painting the walls, ceiling, and window trim white, the owners made two major purchases: a pair of new wicker armchairs to set a country-casual mood and a new area rug for soft comfort and homespun texture. Next, they placed their old piano diagonally in the corner.

To provide more seating, the couple re-covered their old sofa (a garage-sale find) with new red-and-black fabric to complement the wicker chairs. Finishing touches give the room vintage charm. An old pine kitchen table, cut down to coffee-table height, adds the warm glow of well-worn wood, and the refinished oak kitchen stool in the left foreground doubles as tabletop space. In the background, a decades-old bench provides seating at the piano, and an antique lamp serves as a colorful and functional accent piece.

DO YOU HAVE FURNISHINGS YOU WANT TO KEEP?

Nothing adds mellow charm and personality to a room like a few pieces of old furniture. Whether "old" in your case means family heirlooms, garage-sale finds, or a few middle-aged pieces from your basement or attic, pieces from the past can add both a spark of individuality and a homey, lived-in look to your house. And of course every piece of furniture you keep, even if you put some time and money into refreshing it, represents money you didn't spend on a new item.

If you're seriously considering "doing something" about your furniture, the first temptation may well be to throw everything out and start all over again. That's expensive, of course; besides, you might be throwing away some nice things. Given the right kind of treatment, a comfortable chair with faded upholstery, a once-elegant sofa covered with an out-of-date print, and a scarred but still-sturdy table can all become decorative members of a household.

On the other hand, not everything lends itself well to recycling. If you have lumpy chairs, shaky and poor-quality end tables left over from earlier days, or homemade bookshelves that sag irreparably, simple sentiment probably will be your only reason to hold on to them.

There are, however, some good reasons for recycling furniture. Maybe you have a few pieces you're fond of that don't look quite right with more expensive, more recently purchased items; or, perhaps you're looking for ways to renew your old furniture because you have other spending priorities at the moment. (If you're unsure how to go about recycling furniture, see Chapter 9 to learn about slipcovering, reupholstering and restyling, stripping, refinishing, and caning, and Chapter 10 for information about caring for and repairing furniture.)

The elegant room pictured *at left* is an example of one way to reuse furniture. The owners started with three old and mismatched seating pieces—two slipper chairs and an aging sofa. Rather than throw them out and start from scratch, the owners had the sofa and chairs reupholstered to match each other. To further tie the pieces together, the upholsterer added the same button detailing to the chairs' rolled backs and the sofa's rolled arms—a subtle but effective way to "match" the pieces.

How to decide what to keep

Quality counts in used furnishings, just as it does when you're looking for new furnishings in a retail store. Ask yourself: Are tables and chairs sturdy, or do they wobble? Are legs attached securely? Do chairs have braces in corners and stretchers between the legs? Are drawer sides dovetailed? Are drawers varnished but not painted? Are there dust panels between drawers? Do drawers operate easily? Is hardware attached securely?

You may not answer "yes" to each question, but furniture worth keeping is likely to have at least some of these qualities. If the piece passes most of these tests, you can probably remedy other flaws. The main thing is that you like the piece and that it's sturdy.

If you're looking at wood pieces, remember that a cracked or marred finish can be stripped and refinished—even painted. If a chunk of veneer is missing and the piece isn't particularly valuable, you may decide to paint it.

Don't be put off by worn, torn, or frayed upholstery. If the piece is in good shape otherwise, you can make a tie-on slipcover for it in a weekend. Professional reupholstery isn't cheap, but if your used sofa or chair is top quality to begin with, it's probably worth it. Another option: Buy a plain, ready-made slipcover from a department or catalog store, then customize it with a fabric border.

BEGINNING QUESTIONS

WHAT FURNISHINGS FIT YOUR LIFE-STYLE?

When you shop for furniture, focus on your own family. Forget about how your neighbors have furnished their homes, and don't let furniture sales clerks sway you. Think of the furnishings you already have. How well do they complement your life-style? Do you like looking at and living with certain pieces, or are they just there? Formal or informal, old or new, brightly colored or subtle and neutral, your furnishings should reflect your taste, the age and activity level of your family, how much and in what style you entertain—in short, how you live.

Let's start with a simple question: Which room in your home makes you feel the most at ease? Now, think about why you've chosen that room. Probably, its furnishings best reflect your aesthetic and practical needs.

Next, do you have one room you unconsciously avoid? Often, for example, a formal living room is rarely used, while a comfortable, well-worn den serves as family headquarters. If that sounds like a description of your home, it may mean your living room furnishings are incompatible with your life-style.

Regardless of their specific style—traditional, contemporary, and so forth—most furnishings are either formal or informal. You may lean toward one, or a blend of both. Do you favor elegant, sit-down dinners and formal cocktail parties, for example, or are potluck dinners and neighborhood barbecues more your style? Is reading in a wing chair by the fireplace your idea of a relaxing evening at home, or do you prefer to stretch out on a sofa and watch TV?

The slick, modern room pictured *at upper right* offers easygoing comfort as well as striking good looks. Lightweight pieces—a chaise, two upholstered chairs, and chrome-framed Breuer chairs—move easily to allow for changing needs and flexible entertaining. The traditional living room shown *at lower right* is furnished with comfortable classics that suit a more formal life-style. The sofa, carefully placed with its back to the fireplace, defines a cozy seating group.

To find out more about styles, how to work with them, and how to give them your own touch, see Chapter 2—"Furnishing Styles."

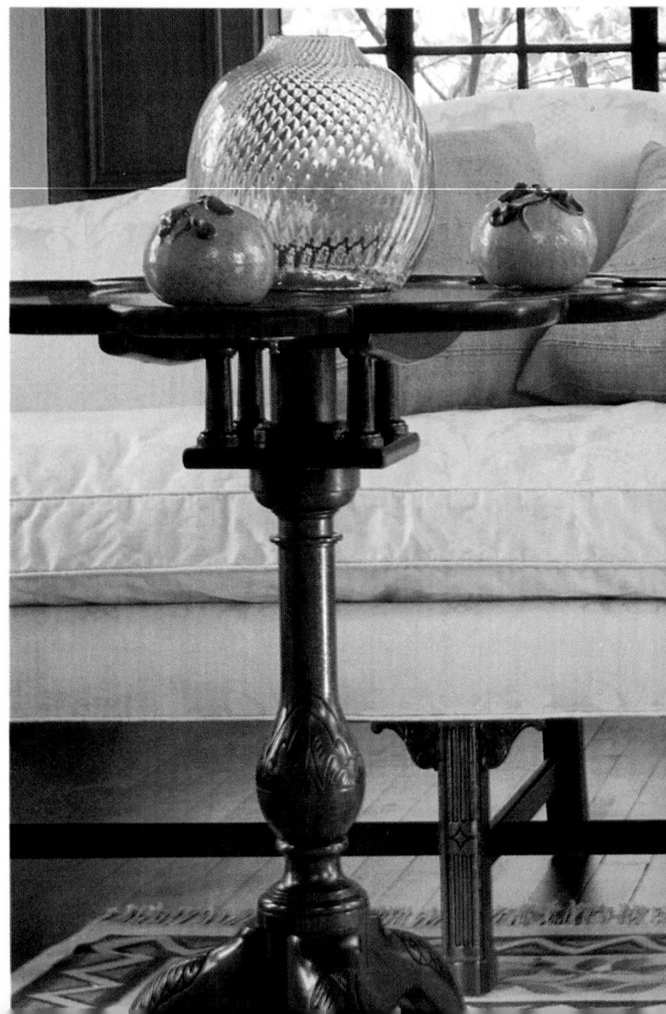

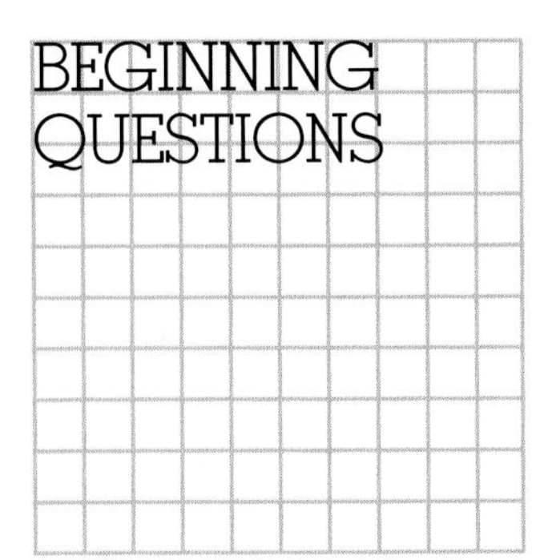

HOW MUCH SPACE DO YOU HAVE?

When it comes to furnishing a room, it often seems that the room has too little or—once in awhile—too much space. Fortunately, a few room-arrangement basics—plus some decorating "tricks"—can make almost any room look and function the way you want it to.

Take a look at the two rooms shown here. One has little space to spare; the other offers almost too much. In each case, clever room arrangements resulted in handsome, inviting living and sleeping spaces. (For more about planning furniture arrangements, see Chapter 4.)

Small-space strategies
If you're faced with less-than-ample square footage, follow a few general rules to make the space seem more generous than it actually is.

• *Pare down.* The fewer furnishings you use, the larger your room will seem. In the room pictured *at left,* a few carefully chosen low-to-the-floor furnishings meet sleeping and storage needs without overpowering the space. Note how storage pieces double as a headboard and a desk.

• *Keep the background simple.* Nothing expands a room's apparent boundaries better than painting your walls and ceilings a light color, as the room shown *at left* illustrates.

• *Use vertical space.* One tall item—an armoire or open-back shelves—will make your room seem taller. (Tall storage pieces also offer lots of room and occupy just a few square feet of floor space.)

• *Float your grouping.* Avoid the temptation to line the walls with furniture. Here, the bed floats in the center of the room, increasing the feeling of spaciousness.

Make the most of oversize rooms
Large rooms can seem cold, austere, and a little intimidating if you don't scale them down to human size. Here are some helpful planning tips:

• *Don't line the walls of large rooms with furnishings.* Move pieces away from the walls to add a feeling of intimacy, as in the room pictured *at right.*

• *Break the room into several groupings.* Instead of one large arrangement of seating pieces, for example, opt for two smaller groupings. Or create one conversation area, then use the remaining space for a small office, music area, or dining space, as in the photo *at right.*

• *Try a fresh angle.* For example, the diagonal tilt of the seating grouping shown *at right* not only helps set it apart from the adjacent dining area, but also breaks up the room's potential boxiness.

• *Consider a dark background.* Patterned wallpaper or a dark paint color on one or more walls will cozy up any large space.

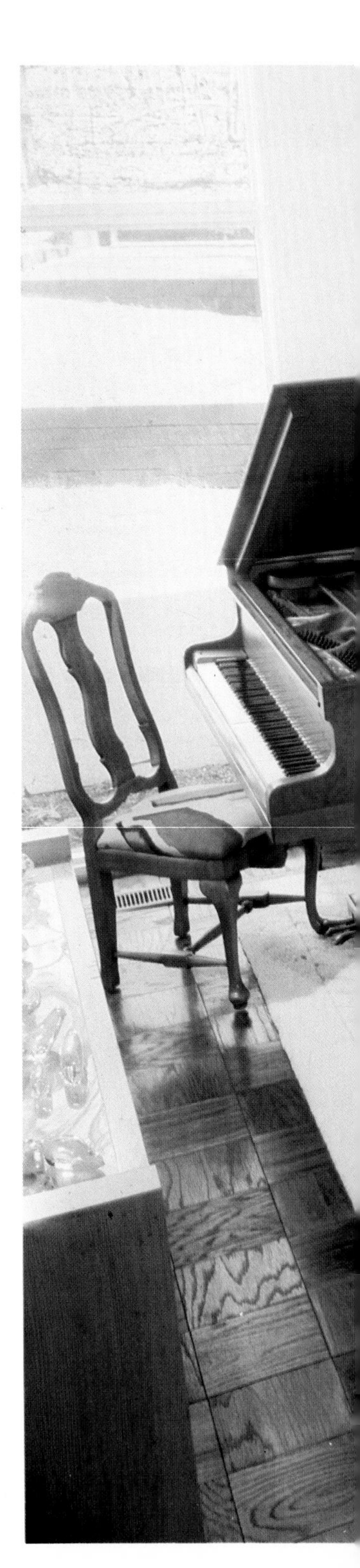

DO YOU PLAN TO MOVE OFTEN?

Nothing is more exciting—and unsettling—than a major move. If you think you'll move often, you'd be wise to plan your furniture purchases with mobility in mind. Choose furnishings that can work well in many rooms and handle a variety of functions. Small-scale pieces are ideal because they can easily fit into almost any space.

When the owners of the rooms pictured here moved to a larger home with larger spaces, their old furniture moved with them. In their first, small living room, shown *below,* an apartment-size sofa teamed with two small, armless slipper chairs to provide ample seating. The seating pieces in the first living room became the nucleus of a new conversation grouping, shown *opposite*, and the round table at the back of the first living room reappears wearing a different skirt and a glass top.

What else moved? If you look carefully at the two photographs, you will see that the handsome dhurrie rug now brightens the dining room adjacent to the living room. The old coffee table and armoire reside in the new home's den (not shown), and the antique pine end table in the photograph *below* serves as a bedroom nightstand (also not shown).

What to look for

Furnishings that will move easily from house to house share certain qualities:

• *Versatility.* Pieces without an obvious label, such as "bedroom," are more likely to fit in from one house to the next. Some furniture is even equally at home on your porch or in your family room; for more about outdoor furniture that can move indoors, see Chapter 7—"Outdoor Furniture."

For versatile indoor furniture, search out simple bookcases and storage chests that can serve in a dining room now, then handle living room or bedroom duties later. Modular storage units, available in many styles, can stack one way now, then break apart and restack when needs alter.

• *Small scale.* Instead of buying one sofa that's 90 or more inches long, opt for a love seat and a couple of chairs, or buy a grouping of modular seating units. You can reshuffle combinations to fit almost any space.

• *Harmonious colors.* You don't have to use an identical color scheme in every room, but variations on the same basic color theme will later enable you to bring together upholstered pieces and accessories from different rooms.

• *Multipurpose furnishings.* Multipurpose pieces are great space-savers, and there's a wealth of them on the market today. In addition to sofa beds that serve for seating and guest sleeping, consider a bookcase with a drop-lid surface that can be used as a desk now and a bar in another home. A wall console that opens to reveal a table is another good choice—it can serve as a handsome hall piece most of the time, then open to offer auxiliary dining or buffet space when and where you need it. (For more about multipurpose furniture, see pages 36-39 and 42 and 43.)

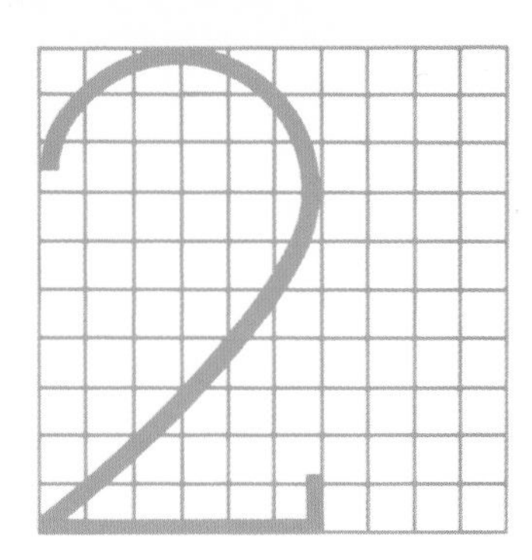

FURNISHING STYLES

When thinking about furnishing a room, most of us have a general idea of the look we favor. Still, we wonder how to select pieces that will pull everything together. Louis XV, Queen Anne, Sheraton, Pennsylvania Dutch, Bauhaus—what do these style labels mean, and how will they affect the way your rooms will look? The answers lie not with the styles themselves, but in the way you use them. This chapter presents five distinct approaches to style: traditional, country, contemporary, casual, and eclectic. Each has its own origins and characteristics. Once you've learned what's special about each, and decided which best suits your family, you'll be well on the way to expressing your style.

TRADITIONAL

Traditional furniture is time-tested furniture; its designs transcend passing fads and blend the best of the past with the needs of the present. Some traditional pieces may actually be antiques; more often, however, they are new furnishings that trace their origins to classic styles of the past—styles that originally were designed and made for the most affluent members of society. Because of this heritage, traditional pieces often have a formal air about them.

Curved legs, graceful carvings, comfortable cushions, and rich, deep colors or soft, flower-garden tints keynote the traditional look. There's nothing harsh or jarring about traditional furniture. Its overall effect conveys a sense of continuity and timelessness. Traditional schemes appeal to families who want their homes to be elegant but not stuffy, comfortable but not too casual.

Perennial classics
A good way to become acquainted with traditional furniture is to learn something about the design periods that contributed to the heritage of these furnishings. Furniture designs spanning several centuries and with roots in many nations are still being reproduced or adapted today.

Two of the best-known historic styles take their names from eighteenth-century French kings—*Louis XV* and *Louis XVI*. Originals of these styles are museum pieces, but French antique furniture has many modern-day descendants, which have been modified to contemporary standards of comfort and construction.

Although the two styles look quite different, both have a formal mien. Furnishings patterned after the Louis XV style feature sinuously curved legs and are often decorated with carvings of shells, leaves, or flowers. Cabinets with curved fronts, called bombé chests, exemplify this style, as do pastel-painted finishes.

Inspired by the classical forms of ancient Rome, Louis XVI furniture is strikingly different. It relies more on straight lines and subdued decoration, graceful proportions, and tapered legs than do the ornate Louis XV pieces.

Eighteenth-century England provided another rich source of inspiration for many items that appear in modern-day traditional settings. The designs, although greatly influenced by French styles, generally are simpler and heavier in scale than their French counterparts.

Some of the most popular English designs originated in the early eighteenth century during the *Queen Anne* period. The reproduction cherry wood highboy, or chest-on-chest, pictured *opposite,* is a classic example of Queen Anne style. Graceful cabriole legs, the broken pediment framing a decorative carved finial at the top, and a general lack of surface decoration give it the understated elegance characteristic of Queen Anne furnishings then and now.

(continued)

TRADITIONAL
(continued)

Other well-known traditional styles with English origins include *Chippendale, Hepplewhite,* and *Sheraton.*

Thomas Chippendale, who worked in the latter half of the eighteenth century, transformed the Queen Anne style into something equally beautiful but more sturdy. His later furniture often had straight square legs, and the chairs featured carved openwork backs.

The designs of George Hepplewhite and Thomas Sheraton were more delicate and finely scaled. Slender legs tapered to a simple spade foot. Instead of carved decoration, exquisite inlays became the norm.

American furniture makers watched England for design trends and copied the styles popular there. Taking advantage of abundant native materials, they used lighter-colored woods such as maple and oak in addition to the dark mahogany and walnut used in England. Many of the simpler American designs have become what we now call "country" furniture. (More about the country style on pages 24-27.)

Preserving the past

By using good reproductions or carefully maintained originals, it's possible to furnish a room that looks much as it might have one, two, or even three centuries ago. In the bedroom shown *above,* an authentic four-poster holds center stage. A well-polished heirloom drop-leaf table adds its own history to the room, and a pair of elegant Oriental rugs contributes to the rich-looking yet welcoming ambience. A room like this, filled with old (or made-to-look-old) furnishings and treasures, creates a sense of peace and history.

Today's traditions

Traditional settings don't *have* to be re-creations of rooms from the past. Traditionally styled furnishings offer great flexibility and blend well with each other. A Chippendale sofa, for instance, goes beautifully with a Queen Anne wing chair.

Consider, too, that your furnishings needn't all be period pieces. Traditional styles can mix comfortably with modern pieces, yet maintain a quiet, period elegance. For example, you can team a modern-day upholstered sofa with traditionally styled side tables and a wing chair and still maintain the timeless sophistication of traditional schemes.

Depending on the furnishings you choose and how you accessorize them, you can create a traditional decor that's elaborate and elegant or one that's cozy and unpretentious.

The airy dining room shown *opposite* draws much of its charm from an antique Sheraton dining table, accompanied by reproduction Queen Anne chairs made to meet the demands of today's family life. The oak strip floor is brightened by a well-worn Oriental rug in rich rust and blue tones. And although traditional details abound—the highly polished woodwork and the small-paned windows, for example—the overall effect is bright and breezy. The floating stairway, undressed windows, and wicker-potted plants all lend a contemporary note to this untraditional traditional room.

FURNISHING STYLES

COUNTRY

Like traditional furniture, country furniture also has roots in the past, but a different past. The original country pieces were made by rural folk who often didn't have the materials—or the expertise—to build elaborate "high-style" furniture like that acquired by wealthy city people. Country, in other words, came from the country.

Country isn't one narrowly defined style. Furniture from just about any region and period can fall into the category of "country" —as long as it evokes the right mood.

Country furniture can be old or new, lovingly copied from a long-ago design or adapted by a modern-day craftsperson. The key elements include rather simple lines, softly polished surfaces, and basic forms that are functional first, decorative second.

Country is at home almost anywhere. The sunlit, polished-pine solarium/bedroom shown *at left* could just as well be in a suburban Cape Cod cottage or a renovated city brownstone. Its mood, however, is country from floor to ceiling and window to window.

The graceful carved bed, rag rug, and bow-back settee are country classics. Lovingly collected accessories, from the child's antique chair and old stuffed bear to the sturdy pottery jug filled with forsythia, add the finishing touches.

What makes a country-style room like this one so appealing? You can select elements that are old, new, or in-between—everything needn't match. The furniture and accessories in a country-style room may have diverse origins, but a common rural heritage, cleanness of line, and hand-hewn quality bind them together. Add to these a blend of natural materials, and you have country.

In place of the mahogany or walnut used to make the fancy furniture of the day, eighteenth- and nineteenth-century country craftsmen used local woods such as maple, pine, cherry, ash, hickory, and butternut. The wood generally was oiled and hand-rubbed to a natural patina. *(continued)*

COUNTRY

(continued)

There's more to country decorating than just the mellow beauty of wood furniture. Natural fabrics, wicker, plants, and flowers often play supporting roles, as in the cozy porch shown *below*. Here a varied basket collection mounted from the rough-sawn cedar ceiling serves as an offbeat focal point for the room, and hanging plants add their own indoor country touch.

This tuxedo sofa is contemporary in style, but its flower-garden print upholstery makes it country in spirit; the wing chair's design predates the sofa's by a couple of centuries. The chair's nubby neutral-tone upholstery is a modern-day version of the fabrics of colonial times.

Where's it from?

Experts usually don't attribute country furniture to a specific craftsman; instead they identify local, regional, even national looks. Some, such as the always-popular Pennsylvania Dutch style, have characteristic decorative features—in this case, brightly painted designs on pottery and furniture. Shaker furniture, on the other hand, is known for its simple lines, natural finishes, and complete absence of decoration; it was often designed specifically to serve dual functions or save space.

For years, manufacturers and individual artisans have copied and adapted both of these styles, as well as others that trace their roots to rural craftsmen. Today's country look borrows not only from these and other styles of the American past, but also from other parts of the world. For example, the dining room pictured *at right* has the feel of a French country house. Reproduction country-French rush-seated chairs and an old French coffee-maker-turned-lamp (on the hutch) set the stage. The circa-1860 American pine dining table and the twentieth-century area rug, with its stylized flower pattern, are homegrown. An antique honey-color hutch brightened with rows of Dresden china adds another Old World touch.

Country comfort

Country decorating—and living—may imply simplicity, but you needn't sacrifice comfort and convenience for a country look. Many surviving older country pieces function as well now as ever, and today's versions often feature easy-care fabrics and finishes. In fact, down-home comfort—visual and physical—is at the heart of country's appeal.

The Last of the
NUBA
by Leni Riefenstahl

FURNISHING STYLES

CONTEMPORARY

When you step into a contemporary-style room, what strikes you first may be the streamlined furnishings, an absence of clutter, and the sleekness of surfaces such as chrome and glass. These elements contribute to a style that looks refreshingly clean. Sink into a body-contoured chaise or a padded-leather-and-chrome chair, and you'll discover that they're pieces designed for comfort as well as style. That's because many creators of contemporary design were inspired by the modernist credo "form follows function." The furnishings fit the human body, and their clean-lined sculptural shapes are free of any extraneous ornament.

In the high-contemporary living room shown *at left,* a monochromatic color scheme lets form and texture take center stage. Balancing the sleekness of chrome and lacquer are warm, natural textures of the upholstery, wooden masks, and plants.

Despite their cool sophistication, the furnishings in this light-filled room invite human interaction. Here, for example, modular seating and storage pieces can be arranged and rearranged to suit the homeowners' changing needs.

Contemporary isn't always formal or without color. In the dining room shown *above,* a brightly woven peasant rug warms up the decorating scheme, contrasting with the tubular steel chairs and the butcher block table. The chairs are adapted from one originally designed in the 1920s by Marcel Breuer of the German Bauhaus School of Art, Architecture, and Design.

Bauhaus designers were among the first to take advantage of newly available materials and manufacturing techniques. If the artisan's touch is absent from contemporary furnishings, it's because they were specifically designed for machine production. The strength and malleability of tubular steel, for example, inspired a totally new support system—Breuer's double-S-shape, which took the place of conventional legs.

(continued)

CONTEMPORARY

(continued)

One of the criteria for good contemporary design is honest use of materials. Nothing is fake or masquerades as something it isn't. In the bedroom pictured *above,* for example, the natural beauty of a bleached wood floor, glossy bamboo furniture, and crisp cotton fabrics give the room its contemporary appeal.

With a plum-and-pastel color scheme and stylized canopy over the bed, this room has a touch of romance that softens the crisp lines of contemporary furniture. However, the spaciousness and lack of surface decorating associated with the furnishing style is still present.

Emphasis on texture

In contemporary furnishings, textural contrast replaces ornamentation as a design element. And in a contemporary scheme lacking brilliant colors or dramatic patterns, texture keeps visual interest high.

The tactile appeal of such things as rough glazed pottery, polished wood, shiny brass and chrome, smooth leather, and slubby silken fabrics is of special importance in a contemporary setting.

Texture also plays visual tricks in a room. A heavily grained wood coffee table, for instance, will appear to take up more space than a sleek plastic laminate one.

The light and airy sitting space pictured *opposite* is proof of the subtle power of texture. A fibrous sisal rug nicely complements the shiny lacquer lamp and sleek mini-slat blinds, and woven wicker contrasts with the icy-smooth chrome-and-glass table. The X-based Barcelona table is a copy of a Bauhaus classic. (The original was designed by Mies van der Rohe and introduced at an exposition in Barcelona in 1929.)

Simplicity by plan

If you want to simplify your life, the refined spareness of a contemporary furnishings scheme can help you get started. Because contemporary rooms are designed for function and versatility, they work well with a minimum of furnishings, which means fewer pieces to take care of. And because contemporary-style furniture is clean-lined and made of easy-care materials, it generally requires minimal maintenance.

CASUAL

Casual furniture is comfortable furniture. Whatever your life-style, and whether you prefer country, contemporary, or traditional styling, you're likely to want at least one room whose main purpose—and look—is relaxing. Easy-care fabrics, cushions that invite you to stretch out with a good book, and eye-pleasing colors—these are the essence of casual decorating. Good casual rooms don't happen casually, however. Like other well-designed rooms, they need careful planning. On these two pages we'll give you some pointers for putting together easy-to-live-in rooms that have a casual flair.

Who wouldn't be comfortable and relaxed in the vibrant family room pictured *at right?* This sun-filled space welcomes snacks, conversation, and good times, with room left over for the family's loom.

In the foreground, a large and comfortable sectional sofa has deep cushions that promise sink-in comfort. The sofa is upholstered with sturdy, stain-resistant fabric. (Yes, you *can* use light colors in a casual room, if you choose the right fabric.)

Adjacent to the kitchen, a natural-wood table doubles for dining and games. The chairs move or fold easily to allow for different groupings and activities. Lightweight, equally mobile baskets serve as end and coffee tables.

Everything about this room invites family and guests to a warm, friendly place. Low-key (though hardly bland) furnishings team with lively but not overwhelming colors for an overall effect that's personal, interesting, and eminently livable.

Suit yourself

When choosing furniture for a casual scheme, first think of comfort. Chairs that invite curling up, lamps that give good reading light, ottomans for resting your legs or leaning against while you sit on the floor—any or all of these may be your idea of comfort. Whether you prefer an old-fashioned rocker or large pillows on the floor, make sure you fit "casual" to your own comfort and tastes.

Both physical and aesthetic aspects are important. A chair that's truly comfortable, for instance, not only feels good to sit in but also adds to the visual appeal and warmth of a room.

Casual is flexible
Successful casual pieces don't demand solo staging. They meld readily into a pleasant, cohesive unit, match your family's needs without fuss, and change to meet changing needs. For example, the sectional sofa shown *at left* works well as a large put-together unit, but it also can be divided to create several smaller, more intimate seating groups.

A double identity is also helpful for casual pieces. If your room performs as a home office as well as a guest bedroom, for instance, opt for a desk that can double as a dressing table and seating that opens up into a bed. Choose flexible storage pieces, such as an old armoire or sleek modular cabinets that can conceal clutter yet provide extra drawer space or hanging space for clothes.

Easy care is a must
Finding furnishings that are both handsome and easy to care for is not as difficult as it once was, thanks to modern technology. Many new fabrics hide their durability behind an elegant facade. Some of the modern soft "suedes," for instance, are actually synthetics that come clean with soap and water. Other fabrics have special stain- and soil-resistant finishes that make even light colors practical.

Many wood furnishings are protected with tough finishes. Polyurethane, for instance, seals wood against dirt, alcohol, and stains. Other furnishings materials, such as various plastics, are naturally durable. They resist stains, spills, even weather, and wipe clean with soap and water.

ECLECTIC

By definition, eclectic decorating borrows the best from all styles. And that means it's potentially one of the most exciting ways to decorate. It also means that you need to plan carefully to keep an eclectic scheme from turning into a catchall of good but mismatched pieces. Make sure you limit your selections to those you really like, and to those that have something, no matter how subtle, in common. You will be amply rewarded by a room that is intriguing both to look at and to live in.

You may find furnishings for an effective eclectic room just about anywhere—in designer showrooms, at out-of-the-way shops in your own town, at elegant auctions or roadside flea markets, even in your attic if you're lucky. In the face of all these choices, you have to be highly selective about elements that are right not only for you but also for each other. Especially when you first start, you'll do best if you keep a few basic principles in mind.

Design and mood

No matter what periods or styles you want to use, choose pieces that are well designed —neither faddish nor interesting only for their shock value. Good design—and its close relative, good taste—needn't be expensive; nor are they necessarily found in any one style of furniture. Function and good looks are what matter, and they're found throughout a wide range of prices and vintages.

When you mix and match pieces, make sure their moods are compatible. For example, the sleek ribbon chair and the dignified grandfather clock shown *at right* are worlds and centuries apart. But because they're both formal, high-style pieces, they bring a sense of distinction to the room they help furnish—and they suit each other's company unexpectedly well.

On the other hand, a rustic wood settee and an elegant Chippendale sofa may have been built in the same year in towns 10 miles apart, but they're not true kin. Both are well designed and in good taste, but one is formal, the other more homespun. This doesn't mean they won't go well together in a skillfully executed eclectic setting, but you're likely to need other pieces and accessories to make the relationship work.

Contrast without conflict

When furnishings from mixed ancestry blend into a cohesive setting, each piece appears all the more individual and unique. In the room shown here, for example, three distinct styles of furnishings function side by side.

The traditional grandfather clock provides the focal point for the arrangement. Its handsome mahogany case and scrolled top embody a design standard of years gone by. The ultramodern ribbon chair is unalterably contemporary, but it shares graceful lines and quiet elegance with the clock. And both the simple pine schoolmaster's desk and the collection of Japanese prints have sufficient design integrity to make them at ease in unexpected company.

Color and pattern

Color can be a useful and unifying force in a room filled with seemingly unlike elements. Choose one color that will predominate, then several others to work as accents. Be sure to repeat each color often enough to tie the furnishings together and give the room a well-balanced look.

As a part of a color plan, you might use the same pattern to link disparate pieces. For example, a bright print upholstery fabric or coordinated toss pillows on both a turn-of-the-century rocker and an early fifties love seat often can meld an otherwise unlikely mix.

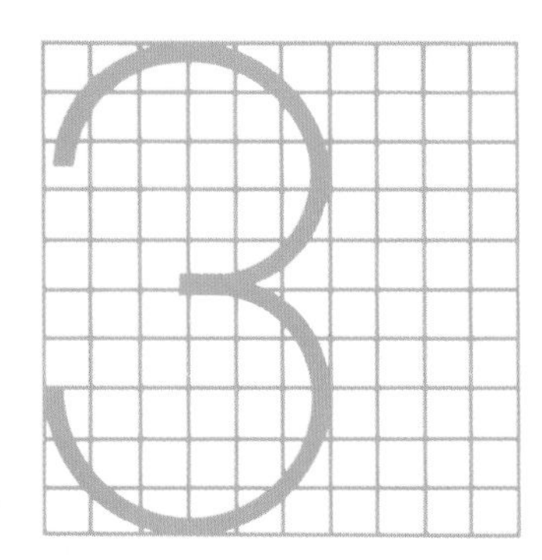

NEW FURNITURE OPTIONS

Like life-styles, furniture use and style no longer are cut and dried. Compact, multipurpose furnishings help homeowners organize and use their space to best advantage. As families demand more out of their living space, rooms will be planned to handle two or three functions, instead of just one. You're more likely to need a living room that doubles as a guest room, or a child's room that sleeps two peacefully. To meet these needs, a wide selection of well-designed furniture makes the most of floor space, and looks great in every role it plays.

SEATS THAT SLEEP

Nearly everyone occasionally faces the problem of having more sleepers than beds. One obvious and long popular solution: the classic convertible sofa. Many sleep sofas offer such good design and comfortable seating that their secret stays well hidden until you need it.

There's a lot more to seats that sleep than convertible sofas, however. Who would suspect that a cocktail table (1), designed as a companion to a modular seating grouping, could make the switch from table to bed in just minutes? (Just lift the hinged tabletop to reveal a fold-out, single bed.) Or that a low-slung foam chair (2) would provide comfortable sleeping with a flip of the wrist? Not only that, but the back cushion of this chair performs a dual function: Unrolled, it functions as padding for the bed; used separately, it becomes an exercise mat.

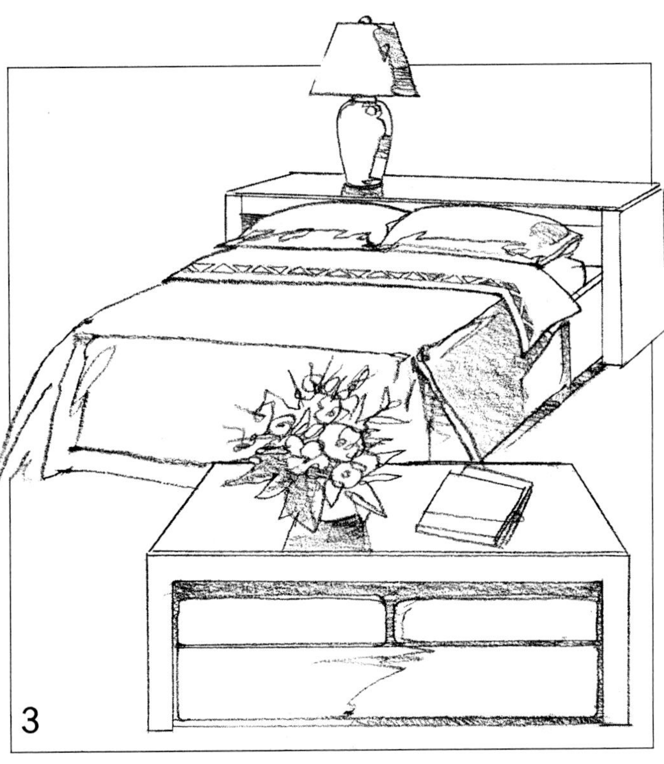

Also among the more innovative convertible sleepers on the market today are fabric-covered tables (3) that house double-width ottomans. For extra seating, you simply pull out the ottoman. If it's sleep space you need, open the ottoman into a comfortable double bed. The backs of the tables are upholstered, giving these pieces added flexibility—they don't need to be used against a wall.

Trim-lined chairs that hide twin-size beds are newly popular as instant guest accommodations (4). Nothing about these sleep chairs is bulky: the tabbed-corner side cushions flip out of the way to provide plenty of pillow space, and a foam seat cushion unfolds into a plump mattress.

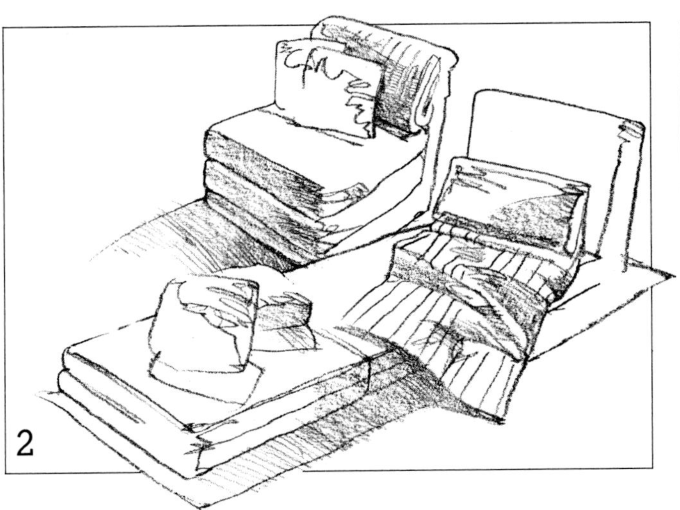

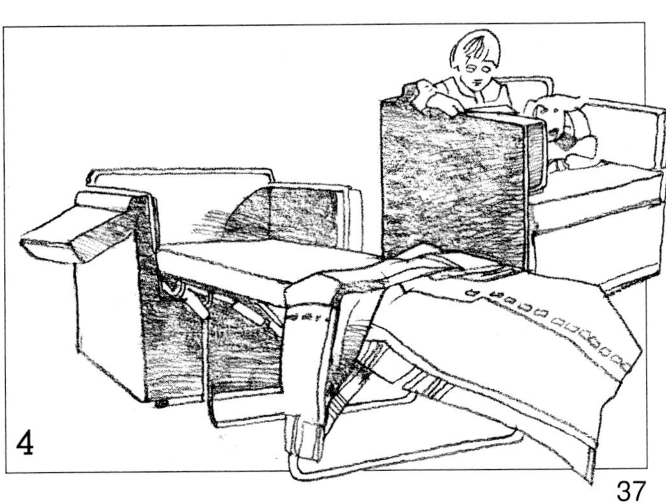

SPACE-SAVING TABLES

1

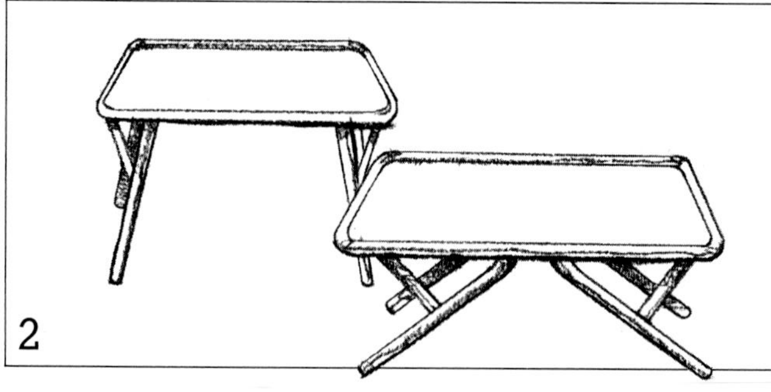

2

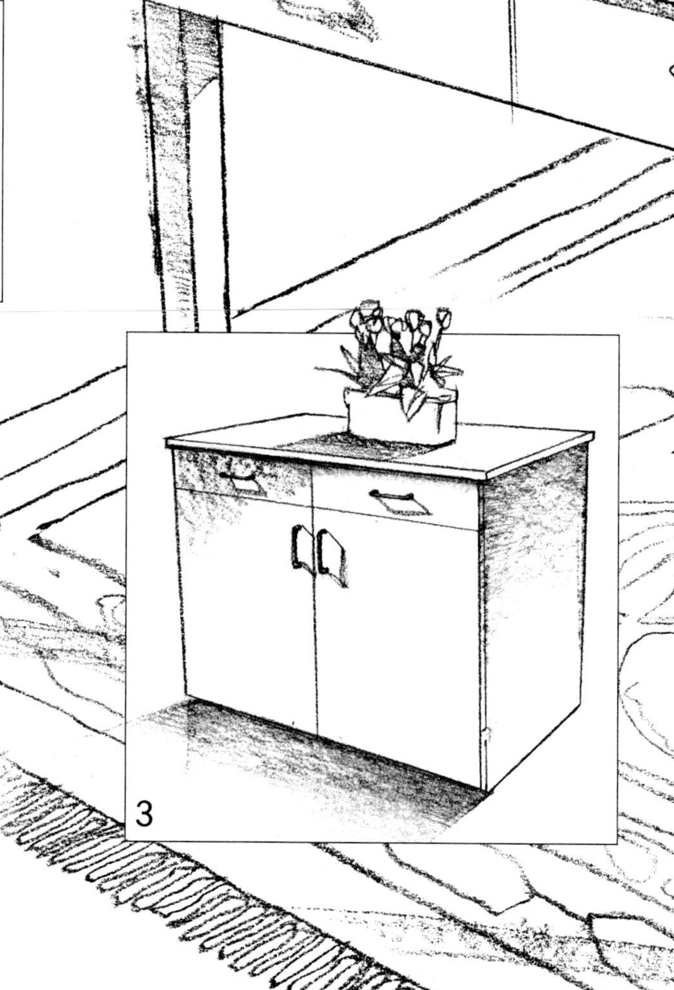

3

One of the easiest ways to create a spacious feeling in a room is to avoid crowding it with large pieces of furniture—especially tables—that see only part-time use. Multi-use folding tables that stretch space in inventive new ways are a perfect answer in this situation.

Some space-saving tables disguise themselves as handsome cabinets; others fold unobtrusively flat for easy storage; and a number of flip-top pieces double in size at meal or party time.

This narrow drop-leaf table (1) can serve as a desk when the leaf is down. When the leaf is up, the table seats four for dinner. Another good space-stretching choice is this collapsible style (2) that adjusts to three heights. By making a few easy adjustments, you can change it from a coffee table to a game table to a dining table—and fold it away for flat, compact storage when you're done.

The streamlined console shown *at right* (3) goes to great lengths to provide a table for dining, work, or hobbies. Four leaves stow away inside. Expanded, the table can seat up to 10 people; folded up, it provides a compact display or serving surface.

Still another innovative option is a convertible console table (4) that conceals four dining chairs. This table stands flat against the wall until dinnertime. Then the leaves are raised and the chairs are pulled out from within to create an attractive dining area.

4

NEW FURNITURE OPTIONS

FURNITURE IN A BOX

Whether you call it quick-assembly, easy-to-assemble, or knockdown (KD), you're probably familiar with unassembled furniture that comes in a carton. KD furniture is made of plastic, wood, metal, or glass, or a combination of several materials.

Whatever the material, you usually need only a screwdriver to assemble it; manufacturers often include small wrenches for tightening bolts when necessary. Equipped with a little basic common sense, even novice do-it-yourselfers can assemble KD furniture in a matter of hours.

The components of even large pieces are compact before they're assembled. One resulting advantage is that you can just go to a store, buy a KD piece, and take it home in your car (or order it through the mail for easy delivery). And because the manufacturer isn't paying someone at the factory to put the pieces together, KD furniture is more affordable than other pieces—at least 20 percent less than if it were preassembled.

KD pieces generally are clean lined and contemporary in styling, although more traditional pieces are available, as are coordinated collections. The bunk bed system shown *at right,* for instance, is available with companion KD seating and storage pieces.

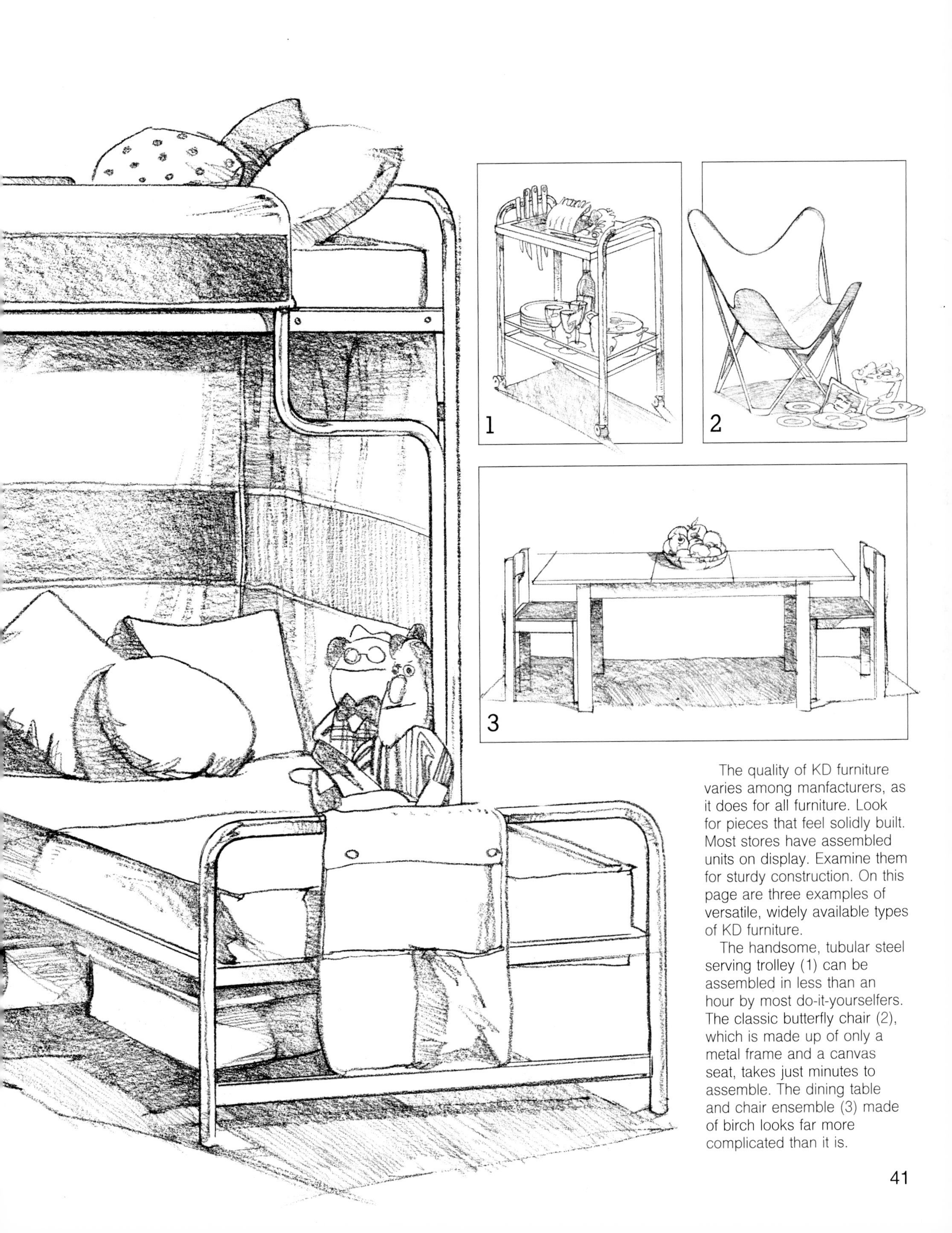

The quality of KD furniture varies among manfacturers, as it does for all furniture. Look for pieces that feel solidly built. Most stores have assembled units on display. Examine them for sturdy construction. On this page are three examples of versatile, widely available types of KD furniture.

The handsome, tubular steel serving trolley (1) can be assembled in less than an hour by most do-it-yourselfers. The classic butterfly chair (2), which is made up of only a metal frame and a canvas seat, takes just minutes to assemble. The dining table and chair ensemble (3) made of birch looks far more complicated than it is.

NEW FURNITURE OPTIONS

CHANGEABLES

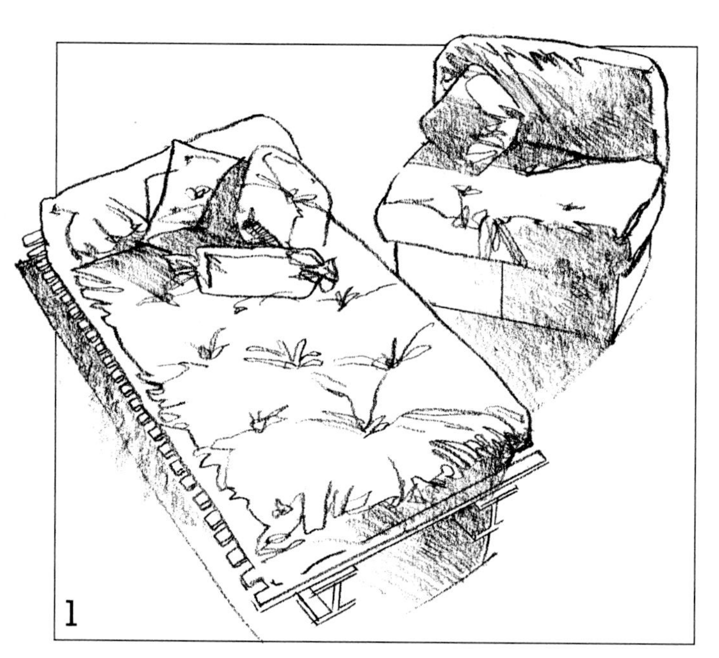

1

2

Furniture that's flexible and easily rearranged provides you with quick ways to change your interior landscapes.

One of the most versatile pieces you can buy is a *futon* (1). These cotton mattresses have served as beds in Japan for centuries and have recently made their way to the West. A futon can lie flat for sleeping, fold against a wall, or change into a low-slung chair. You can place a futon directly on the floor, but for more comfort, raise it on slatted wooden bed, sofa, or chair frames. Futons are excellent choices for any living area where space is at a premium. They also work well in kids' rooms, where they double as lounge pieces.

Flexibility is a plus for storage. With modular storage units (2) you get display and storage space—and the chance to choose the configuration you want—with drawer units, open shelves, cabinets, or even a pull-down desk.

When you furnish a room for a child, keep in mind that children grow—and grow quickly. Their sleeping and storage needs change, too. The crib-and-chest combination (3) shown *below*, for example, matures along with a child. At first perfectly at home in a nursery, it later changes into a single bed with storage drawers below and a three-drawer nightstand.

3

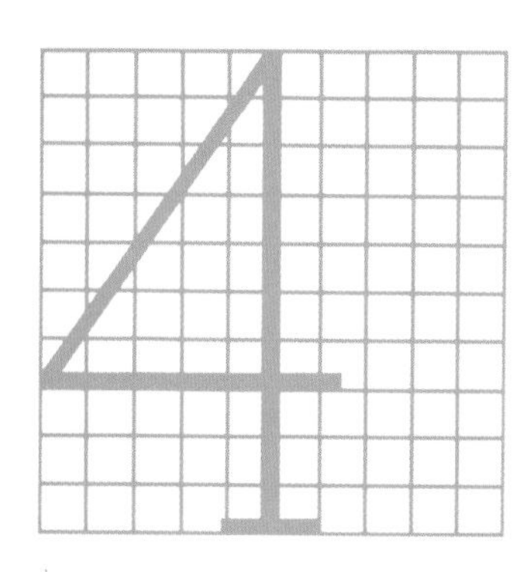

ARRANGING YOUR FURNITURE

Stymied by a room that has attractive furniture but doesn't quite seem to work? Maybe all you need to do is turn the sofa 90 degrees or move a table to the other side of the room. Or maybe the scene needs a complete reorganization. Whatever your problems arranging furniture, help is on the way. This chapter takes you on a tour of problem-solving rooms, tells how to think and rethink your room schemes, and presents a series of templates so you can work out your ideas on paper first.

ROOM-ARRANGING BASICS

How you arrange furniture in a room depends on three major factors: what you want the room to do, the space itself, and how people move through it.

- First, consider the room's *function*. For example, are you planning a room primarily for adults, or a place for the entire family to gather?
- Next, think about the *architecture* of the space itself. How high is the ceiling? Where are the doors and windows? Does the room have a focal point, such as a fireplace, that you want to emphasize? Or would you rather face away from a window with a bad view?
- Finally, consider the room's *traffic patterns*—the natural flow of people into, out of, and sometimes through the room. The patterns have a lot to do with how you arrange your furniture. Ideally, those traffic lanes should be two feet or more wide and should skirt major conversation groupings.

The arrangement of furniture in the living room/solarium shown *at right* reflects all three considerations. The homeowners wanted to maximize an open feeling, yet maintain each room's separate identity. A large archway serves as a clear-cut boundary between the two spaces. And the living room furniture was placed so people can move easily to other parts of the house.

Matching upholstery and the same wall color in both spaces tie the two rooms together visually. Still, the arrangement of the furniture itself lets the two rooms function independently, which facilitates traffic movement. To keep conversation distances comfortable and give everyone a view of the fireplace (at extreme right in photo), the living room furniture grouping floats in mid-room.

(continued)

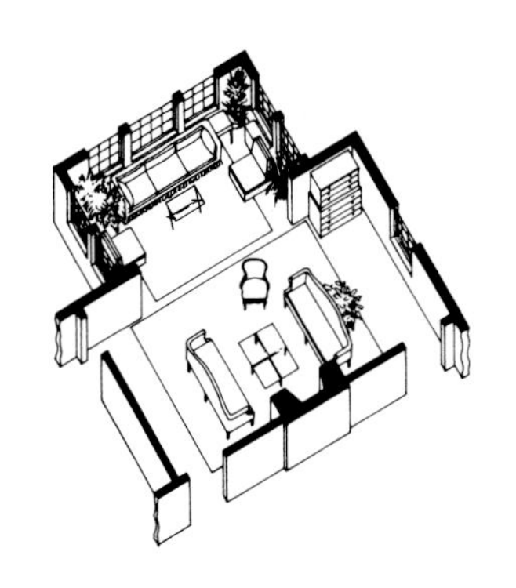

GASTON DIEHL · THE MODERNS

KITCHEN

ROOM-ARRANGING BASICS

(continued)

Once you know how you want a room to function, what its natural architectural features are, and how traffic will flow through it, the time has come to reshuffle furniture. To save wear and tear on your body and on your furniture, however, preplan your arrangement the easy way—on paper. By experimentally positioning and repositioning your furnishings with templates, you can try lots of new ideas before settling on the best arrangement. A paper plan also can help you create a balance of furniture sizes, as well as colors and patterns, throughout your rooms.

Drawing a plan

Start with a sheet of ¼-inch graph paper and let each square represent one foot. Carefully measure your room and sketch its outline on the graph paper as shown *at right.* Be sure to indicate windows and doors (and the directions in which they swing), all electrical outlets, telephones and telephone jacks, light switches, the cable television entry point, and even furnace vents and cold-air returns in the floor and walls. Also indicate any architectural features, such as a fireplace, an archway, or built-in bookshelves.

Now note the room's traffic patterns on the plan, using lines and arrows; allow at least 2 feet (two graph paper squares) for each lane. (You can change the traffic lanes later as you position your furnishings.) Leave at least a 3-foot clearance at all interior doorways, and try to allow 4 feet at an entry door.

To give your groupings added interest, try to find a logical focus for each. If you don't have an obvious one—such as a fireplace, a picture window with a good view, or built-in book and display shelving—don't despair. You can create a focal point. For example, an unusual window treatment, an eye-riveting gallery wall, or a special storage unit would work well. Once you've found your center of interest, play it up by arranging your furnishings around it.

Begin your plan

Now you're ready to trace and cut out the templates provided on pages 52-53, 60-61, and 66-67. Use the templates that come closest to the size and shape of your own furniture items. Width and depth are indicated on each template. Unless you have a space problem, don't worry if your furniture differs by 2 or 3 inches from our templates; if space is critical, or if you can't find a template for one of your pieces, make your own template out of graph paper, remembering that ¼ inch represents 1 foot.

You may want to color the templates with felt-tip markers to help color-coordinate arrangements as we've done, *above right.* With samples of carpets, wall coverings, paints, and upholstery patterns, you can get a good idea of how patterns, textures, and exact colors are mixing.

Remember balance and scale

You'll probably find it works best to place your largest pieces on the plan first. As you arrange the furniture, keep visual balance in mind, so all your heavy-looking or tall pieces don't end up on one side of the room.

Although varying the scale of items can add interest, be sure not to overpower a small item by placing a large one beside it. Instead, aim for harmony by balancing two or more small items against a large one.

Tables and lamps should be in proportion to—and within easy reach of—the sofas and chairs they serve. A sofa with a high arm requires a high end table so a person sitting on the sofa can reach it easily without having to lean over the arm. Conversely, a low-line or armless sofa or chair will need a low end table, both for convenience and eye-pleasing scale.

Be sure all table lamps are up high enough to shed maximum light, yet low enough to avoid glare. Check floor lamps, too, to see that they do not block views in conversation groupings or present an overhanging, head-bumping hazard to the person sitting nearest them. Lamps and tables need to be in proportion to each other, too. A massive lamp, for example, will dwarf a tiny end table (which, by the way, may not be sturdy enough to hold the lamp safely).

Planning for people

The relation between table height and chair height differs depending on what you use the table for. Dining tables typically measure 29 inches high and usually require a chair with an 18-inch seat height. A game table, on the other hand, is 25 inches high and requires a lower seat height, as well as additional leg room around it. End tables usually are 19 to 22 inches high, and coffee tables from 15 to 18 inches high. Your choice within this range depends largely on the height of your seating pieces.

For comfortable conversation groupings, try to seat about six persons within 8 feet of each other. More than six people in an area that size will seem crowded, and additional space will diminish the intimacy of a group arrangement.

When you position your furnishings, be sure to allow space for people to get into and out of groupings. That means you'll want at least 15 inches of leg room between a sofa or chair and your coffee table and at least 3 feet of space around the perimeter of a dining table.

CASE STUDY: A WALK-THROUGH ROOM

Even the best-designed house is likely to have at least a few rooms where doors and walkways create less-than-ideal traffic patterns. When walking through a room is like negotiating an obstacle course, or when the main path to another part of the house divides a conversation grouping, a carefully planned furniture arrangement can help rid those problems.

A small space is likely to suffer from inconvenient traffic patterns even more than a large space. The diminutive condominium shown here originally had little visual interest, and posed a classic room-arrangement problem: The entry (see plan) funneled traffic either directly into the kitchen or diagonally across the dining area to the living area and bedroom hallway.

This versatile living/dining space, photographed from two angles, illustrates one good way to deal with a walk-through room.

The first step is to create a seating area that traffic won't interrupt. To do that, this owner grouped a sofa and two chairs at one end of the room, *above,* then used a colorful Oriental runner over the wall-to-wall carpet to set the conversation area clearly apart from the adjacent traffic lane. Now, there's a well-defined path for people to walk through the room, and the resulting seating group is cozier and more inviting than if the pieces were spread out around the walls.

The floor-to-ceiling shelves help, too; they consolidate books and stereo gear against the walls, thus minimizing intrusion into traffic patterns. The shelves provide a library backdrop for the living area, further defining that section of the room.

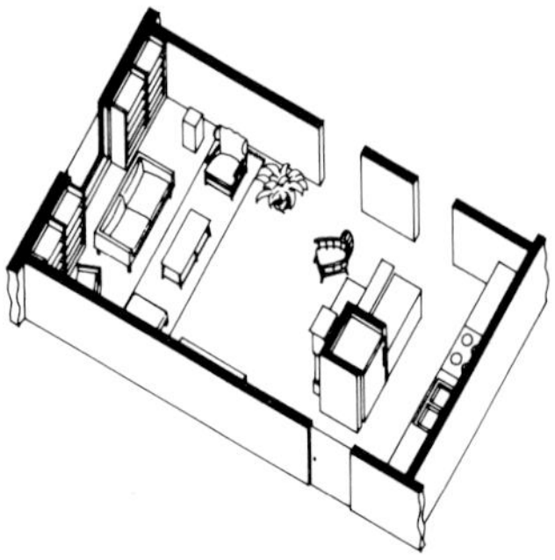

Table for two—or more

The view *opposite* shows how a slim wooden gateleg table and handsome Windsor chair can meet several needs. When the leaves are folded down as shown, the table fits neatly along the wall, conserving precious floor space. When it's time for dinner, the leaves come up and folding chairs come out from a nearby closet. The result: ample part-time dining space for four, with not a traffic jam in sight. Or the owner can open up just one leaf to create dining room for two or a spot for bill-paying and letter-writing—all without blocking access to the kitchen.

CASE STUDY: A CUT-UP ROOM

An unbroken expanse of walls is a reliable backdrop for furniture groupings, but what do you do when doors and windows cut up a room's walls? The answer: Pull furnishings away from those openings to create interesting groupings and new room dimensions.

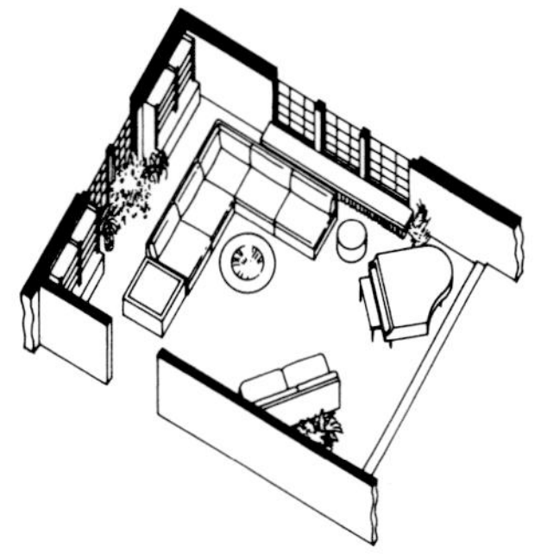

At first glance, this spacious and inviting room looks virtually problem free. Lots of windows and a pair of gracious French doors provide abundant light and architectural interest. But all those window and door openings have their drawbacks. This living room not only has little wall space for furniture to back up against, but, like many cut-up rooms, it also has to accommodate heavy traffic. Here, for example, to get to and from the front door, the stairway to the second floor, the adjacent dining room and kitchen, and the solarium (see plan), you have to pass through the living room.

For maximum flexibility, the owners chose modular furnishings and created a floating triangular seating arrangement. The two armless pieces in the foreground focus attention on the larger, L-shape seating configuration by turning their backs on an adjacent dining space. A small grand piano, also set at an angle, provides another boundary.

The arrangement shown here blocks access to the solarium, but in warm weather, the plants go into the solarium and the seating pieces pull forward to allow passage through the French doors.

Whether or not complex traffic patterns are involved, a floating furniture arrangement is a good solution in rooms whose walls are broken up by many openings.

One drawback of floating arrangements is the hazard of electric cords strung across the floor. To avoid this, consider ceiling-mounted track lighting or an attractive ceiling fixture. Or have an electrician install floor plugs for conventional lamps.

TEMPLATES: UPHOLSTERY AND BEDDING

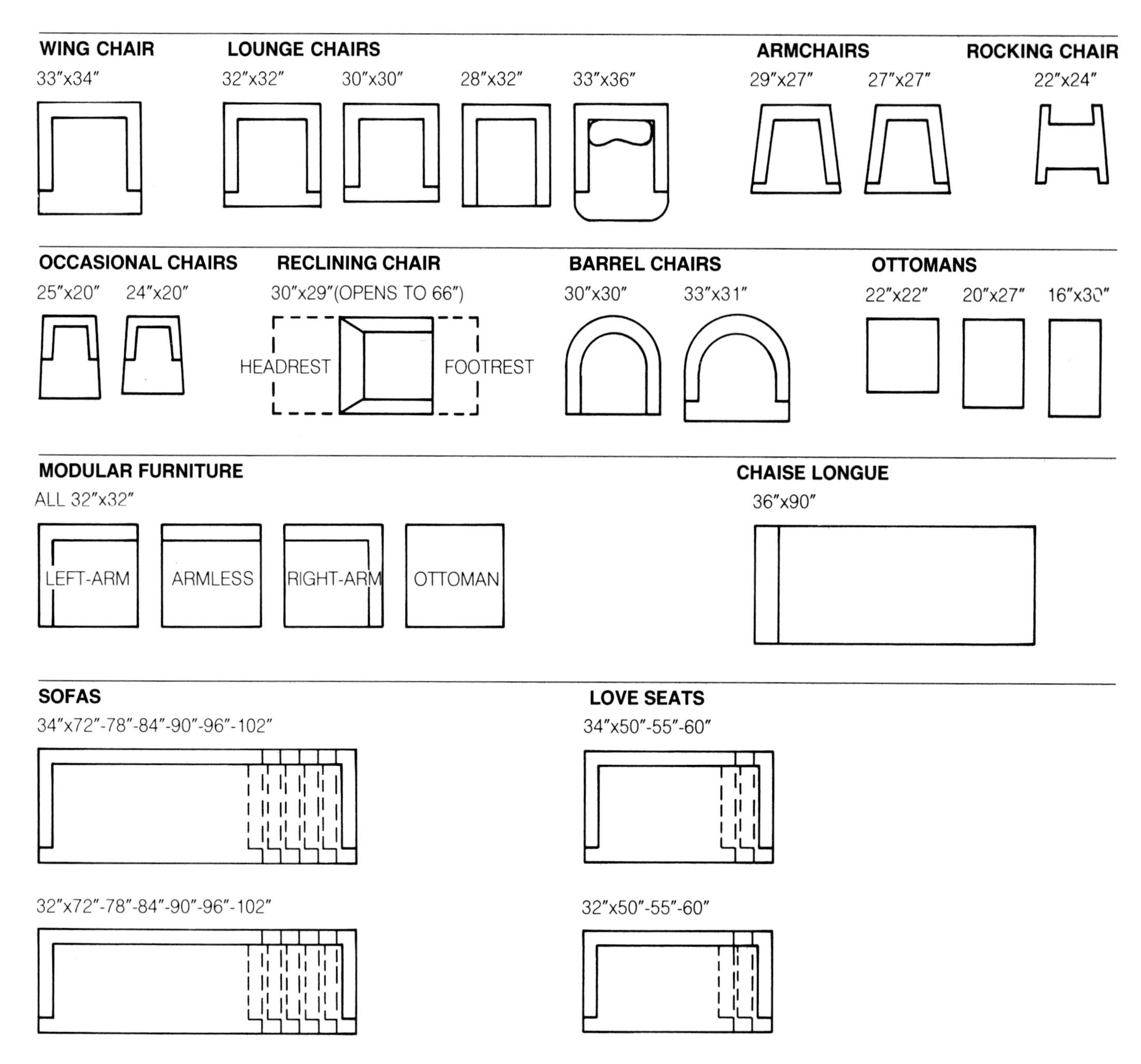

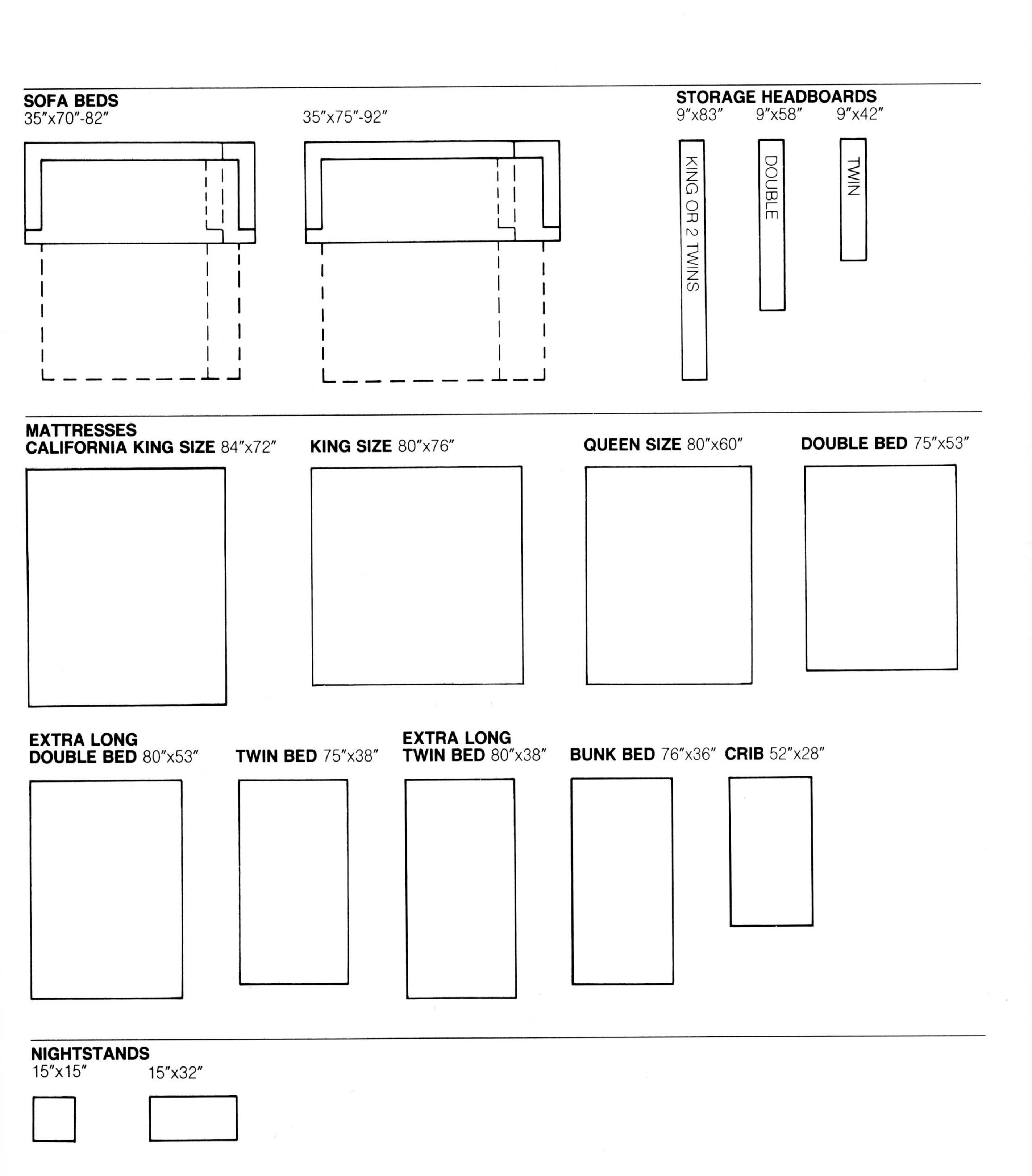
SOFA BEDS
35"x70"-82"
35"x75"-92"
STORAGE HEADBOARDS
9"x83"
9"x58"
9"x42"
KING OR 2 TWINS
DOUBLE
TWIN
MATTRESSES
CALIFORNIA KING SIZE 84"x72"
KING SIZE 80"x76"
QUEEN SIZE 80"x60"
DOUBLE BED 75"x53"
EXTRA LONG
DOUBLE BED 80"x53"
TWIN BED 75"x38"
EXTRA LONG
TWIN BED 80"x38"
BUNK BED 76"x36"
CRIB 52"x28"
NIGHTSTANDS
15"x15"
15"x32"

CASE STUDY: A ROOM FOR TWO CHILDREN

For kids of all ages, sharing a room means allowing for double storage, play, hobby, homework space, and—perhaps most important—privacy. Here are some doubling-up suggestions. Use them as is, or adapt them to the ages and personalities of the room-sharers in your own household.

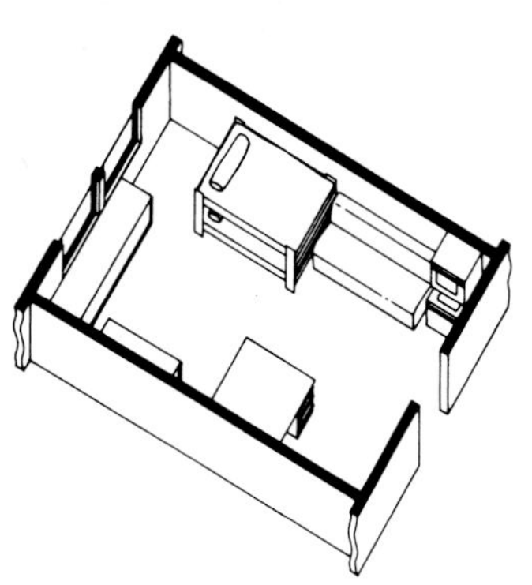

When two children share a room, every inch of space becomes precious. So, the room must have as many space-saving tricks in it as possible.

- For example, stacked bunk beds, such as those shown *at left,* sleep two in the space of one, and tall metal shelves corral lots of kids' stuff without taking up much floor space. This arrangement maximizes the amount of open area available for active play. A furniture arrangement like this works well for children who are close in age and get along well together.
- For children separated by more than a few years, or for children with different play habits, more privacy may be a good idea—a necessity, in fact. Using the tall shelf unit to divide the room into two spaces, one for each child, is one way to achieve this.
- Another possibility would be to place a tall, solid storage unit between the sleep area and the shared play area, allowing an older child to read, study, or play quietly while the younger one sleeps or rests.

Because children's needs and wants change so often and so rapidly, it's a good idea to build as much flexibility as possible into any child's room. These bunk beds can be separated for use in different rooms or parts of the same room as the children get older. The white drawer units can form two work desks in each child's private "zone." Even the roll-around stools have a double identity—they're really storage bins that can stack atop one another when their casters are removed.

Other two-in-one solutions, not shown here, include trundle beds, high-rise platform beds with drawers underneath, and sleeping lofts.

CASE STUDY: A MASTER BEDROOM RETREAT

Whether your bedroom is small or large, a well-planned room arrangement can turn it into something more than a sleeping place. If the room is spacious, use a divider to create a separate sitting area, home office, exercise center, or dressing room. Even if your space is less than grand in scale, you still may be able to carve out a small reading area with the help of a comfortable chair and a lamp. Here are some tips.

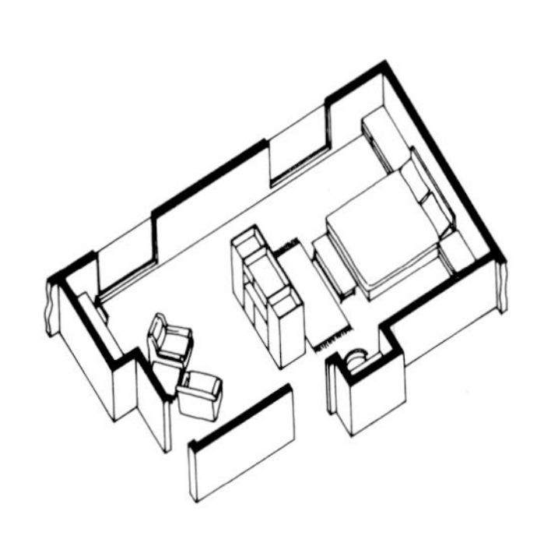

In this long, narrow master bedroom, a floor-to-ceiling divider, *left,* creates two separate and better-proportioned spaces—one for sleeping, the other a cozy sitting-spot-for-two. The divider provides storage space and houses a TV set on a swivel shelf that turns for TV viewing from either side.

At the sleeping end of the room, *opposite,* wall-mounted bedside tables and reading lamps save floor space; at the room's other end, enough space remained for a couple of lounge chairs, *above.*

Even if yours is a *really* small bedroom, you probably can find a corner for a comfortable chair and a slim floor lamp or wall-hung light. With just a little more space, you can do even more. For example, if you haven't room for a boxy divider like the one shown, consider using a folding screen or hanging a mini-slat blind or shirred curtain panel from the ceiling. Another option is a low-level divider, such as two or three low modular storage chests lined up against the foot of the bed; such a divider can store clothing inside and a television set on top. And you still may have room beyond it for a favorite chair and ottoman.

Word People

CASE STUDY: A HOME OFFICE

"Working at home" once may have been a polite way to say you were taking a spring day off to watch the daffodils grow, but now it means business. And that means more and more people are looking for work space in their homes—room for efficient furniture and communications tools that range from a typewriter and stationery to a computer terminal and printer. Here are some room-arrangement pointers to consider.

One prime candidate for a home office is likely to be your basement, a part of the house whose usual isolation makes it ideal for non-household-related activities. Even if another part of your house—be it attic, spare room, walk-in closet, or alcove—is a better choice in your case, the modular basement office shown here will give you ideas for planning your own work space.

The owner, an art dealer, needed a simple, well-lighted, gallery-like space where she could work alone or confer with clients.

Furnished with mobile and modular pieces, this office has seating for clients and lots of shelf and desk space. Each piece is small enough to fit into a compact space but can combine with others to meet more complex needs. The laminated Parsons table works for solo research and for consultations. The roll-around desk chair and several stools go wherever needed.

This basement work center illustrates an important point about creating a home office: When recycling domestic space for work use, you may have to deal with awkward or irregularly shaped and sized spaces. If traditionally scaled furnishings don't fit, it may be a fairly simple—and highly worthwhile—task to custom-fit a work surface or storage unit.

The desk is testimony to careful planning—it rests on a file cabinet in the corner, then angles out atop a print drawer unit. To raise the drawer unit to its proper height, the owner built an open wooden box. Besides serving as support, the box also provides useful additional storage.

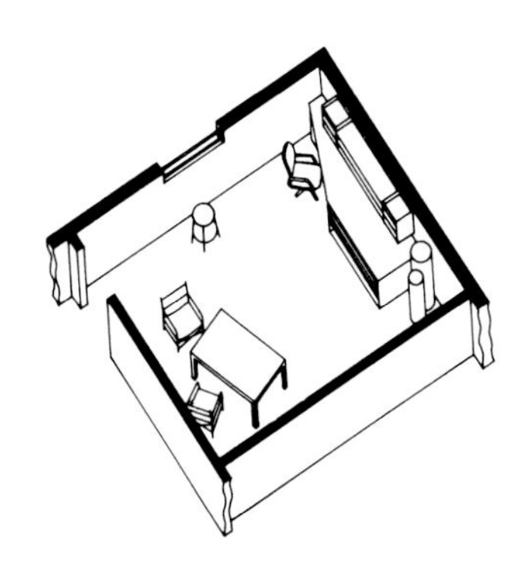

ART NOW
HISTORY OF MODERN ART
DAVID HOCKNEY BY
RICHARD LINDNE
THE NEW YORKER ALBUM OF DRAWINGS 1925-197

TEMPLATES: OCCASIONAL TABLES, DESKS, AND SPECIAL PIECES

NESTING TABLES

16″x24″

TABLES

14″x20″ 16″x22″ 16″x25″ 16″x27″

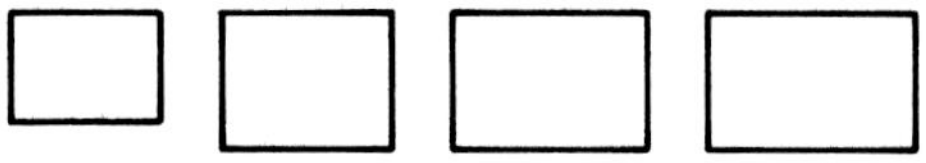

SOFA TABLES

15″x60″ 22″x66″

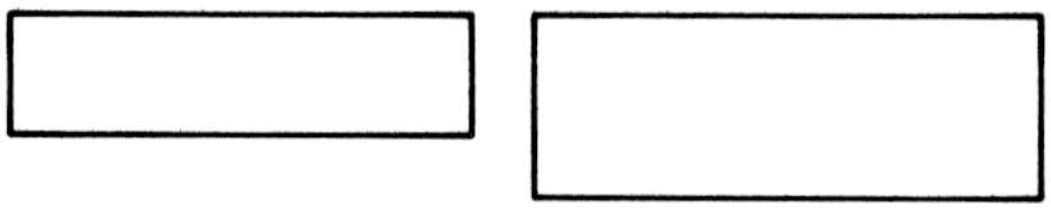

COCKTAIL TABLES

20″x60″ 20″x66″ 22″x44″ 22″x54″ 22″x60″

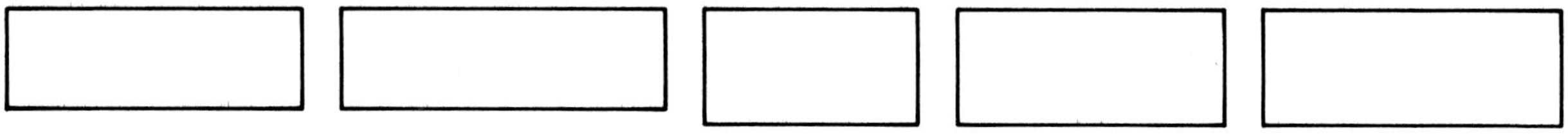

22″x70″ 24″x58″ 28″x66″ 32″x66″

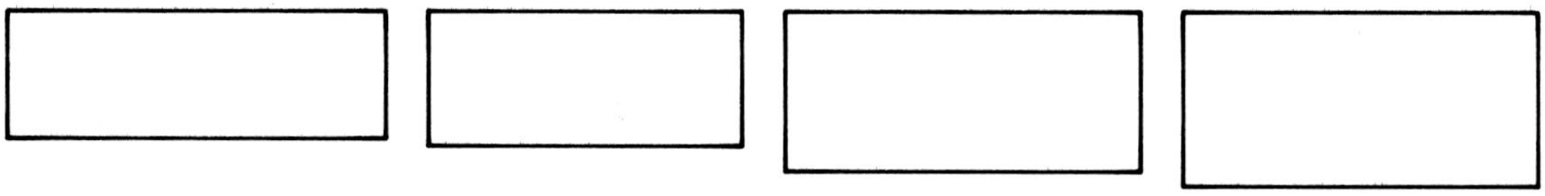

HEXAGONAL COMMODES OR TABLES

40″ 36″ 32″ 30″ 28″ 24″ 20″

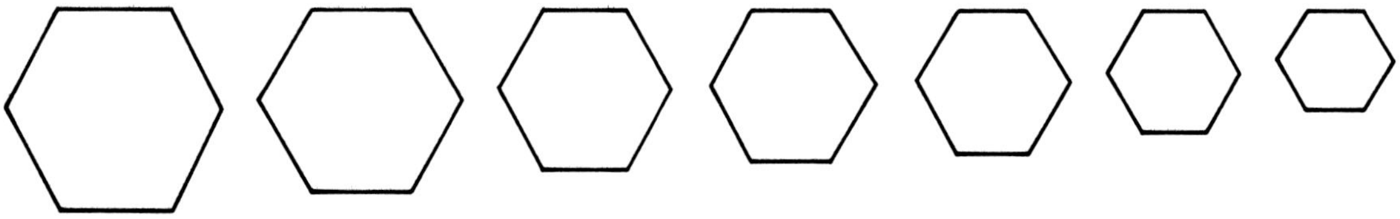

SQUARE TABLES

36″ 28″ 24″ 20″ 18″

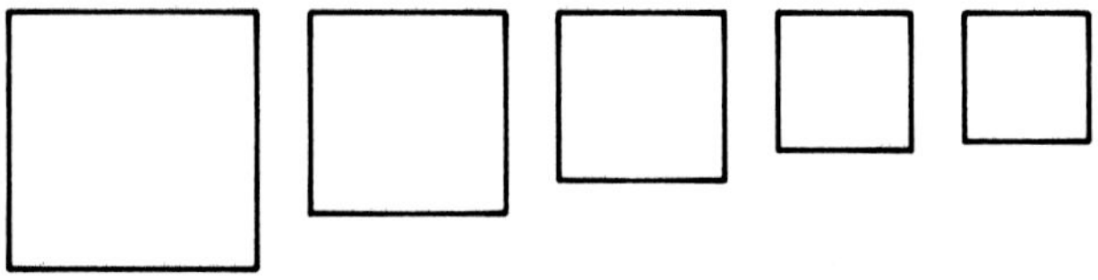

CARD OR GAME TABLE

32″x32″

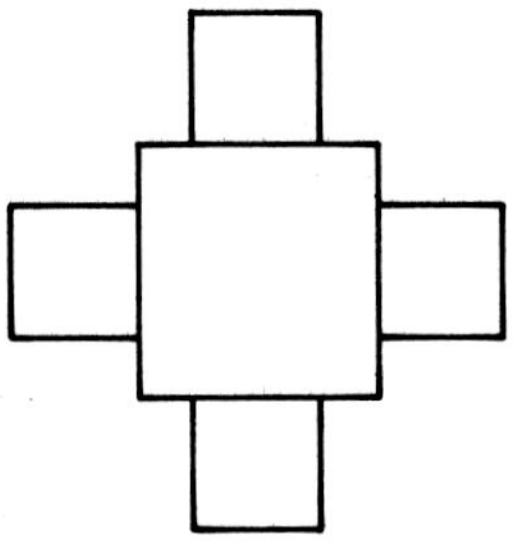

16″x16″

ROUND TABLES

40″ 36″ 24″ 18″ 12″

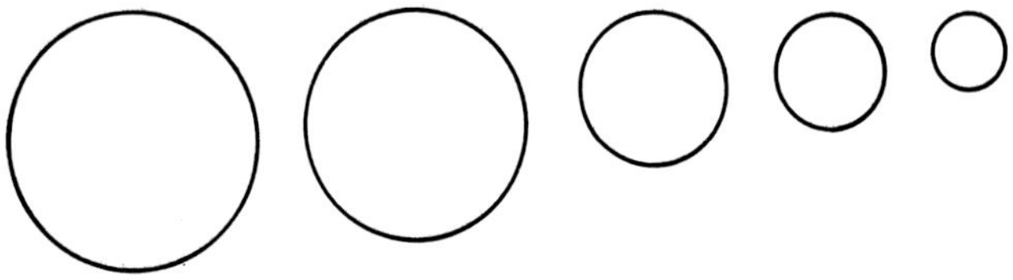

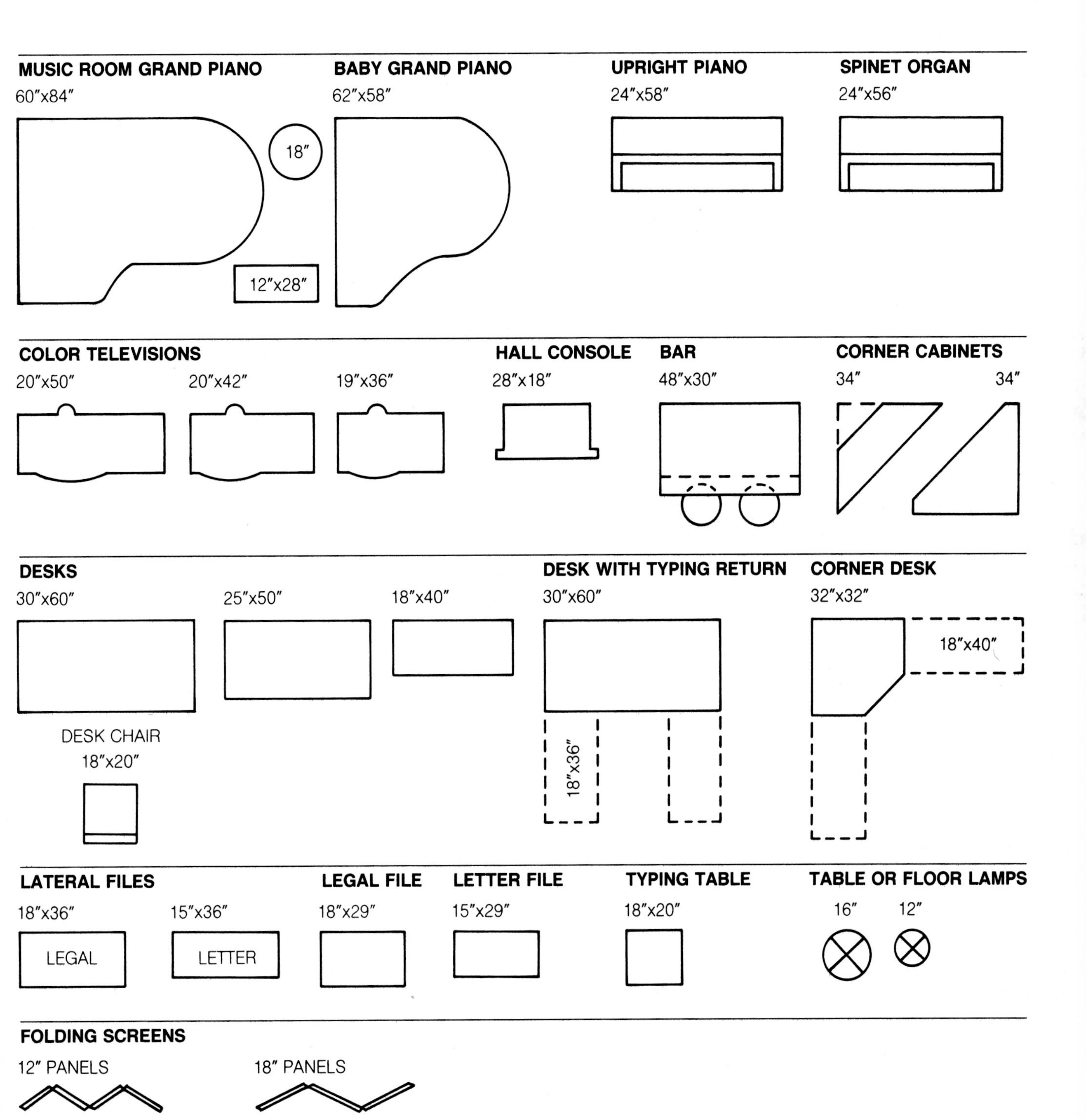
MUSIC ROOM GRAND PIANO
60"x84"
18"
12"x28"
BABY GRAND PIANO
62"x58"
UPRIGHT PIANO
24"x58"
SPINET ORGAN
24"x56"
COLOR TELEVISIONS
20"x50"
20"x42"
19"x36"
HALL CONSOLE
28"x18"
BAR
48"x30"
CORNER CABINETS
34"
34"
DESKS
30"x60"
25"x50"
18"x40"
DESK CHAIR
18"x20"
DESK WITH TYPING RETURN
30"x60"
18"x36"
CORNER DESK
32"x32"
18"x40"
LATERAL FILES
18"x36"
LEGAL
15"x36"
LETTER
LEGAL FILE
18"x29"
LETTER FILE
15"x29"
TYPING TABLE
18"x20"
TABLE OR FLOOR LAMPS
16"
12"
FOLDING SCREENS
12" PANELS
18" PANELS

CASE STUDY: LIVING IN ONE ROOM

One-room living just may be the ultimate challenge to ingenious furniture arrangements. Whether you're furnishing an apartment for yourself or simply making a room in your home do more jobs, the right furniture, arranged properly, can help you use every inch.

In a single room, first determine the functions you want it to serve, then separate them with furniture groupings rather than walls.

Here, in a small apartment, seating and sleeping fit into the cozy, denlike alcove shown *above.* The colorful L-shape seating unit consists of twin mattresses on homemade plywood-box frames. For daytime camouflage, fitted sheets "upholster" the mattresses, and colorful pillowcases dress up ordinary bed pillows. Framing the sleep/seating unit are a bookcase on one end and a white cube on the other. Both provide much-needed storage. Wall-mounted swing-arm lamps save floor space.

Underfoot, a sisal rug sets the alcove apart from the nearby dining area shown *at right.* Here, four chairs nestle around a skirted table. The chairs' open styling keeps them from overpowering the small space. Because they're lightweight, they are easily carried to the "den" when needed. And an airy, lightweight, Bauhaus-inspired lawn chair (a secondhand find) moves from the living to the dining area for extra mealtime seating.

To augment your space-conscious furnishings, choose a wall-hugging window treatment. Streamlined shutters like those shown *above,* Roman shades, or mini-slat or vertical blinds provide optimum light and air control without taking up much space.

Mirroring a wall is another space-expanding ploy that's easy to do. The mirrored wall shown *at right* not only adds needed dimension, it also creates a pleasant window-like view on a plain wall.

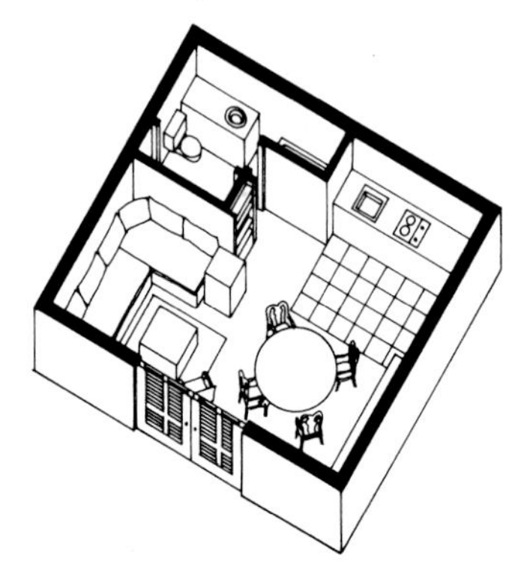

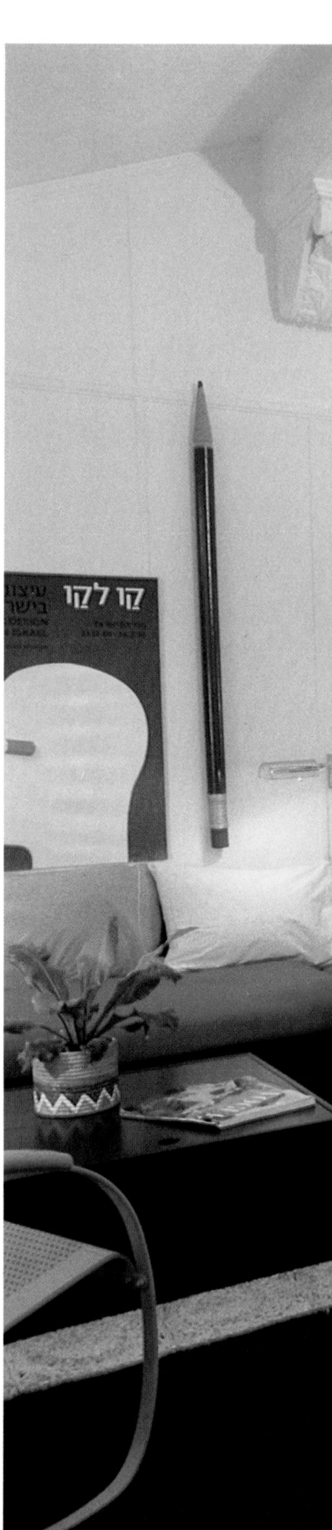

CASE STUDY: A MULTIMEDIA FAMILY ROOM

Is the clutter from electronic games and audio and video gear threatening to take over your family room? Sophisticated new entertainment equipment has become part of the leisure-time activities of many families. But finding room for it in heavily used family rooms may be more of a challenge than some of those fast-action games themselves. Read on to find out how you can bring your own family room into the electronic age without feeling as if you live in a toy store or audio center.

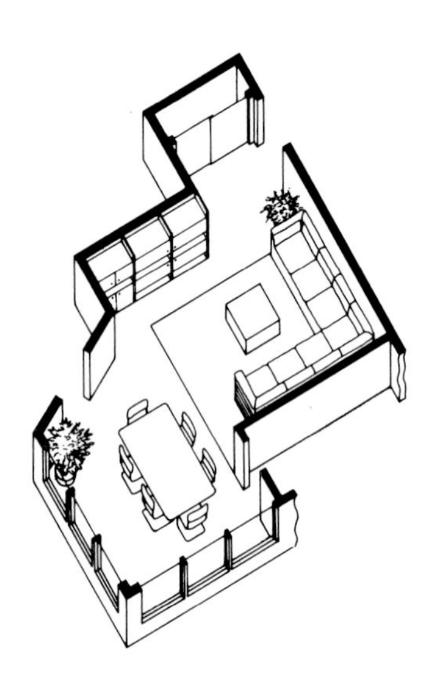

This comfortable family room just off a kitchen accommodates all the usual paraphernalia of modern-day family entertainment: books, TV, stereo equipment, and games. A sturdy, spacious wall system that cleverly conceals much of the electronic gear is key to the successful scheme.

The streamlined, floor-to-ceiling storage units combine open display shelves, used to show off family collections and books, with closed compartments for stereo components, games, and other often-used items. Bifold doors just below the video cassette recorder open to reveal the family's television set.

In addition to handling a multitude of storage needs, your family room should be an inviting spot for relaxation and casual entertaining. Here, durable seating units are arranged in a cozy L for sink-in, feet-up comfort. The laminated cube that serves as a coffee table also is a compact storage spot for bar supplies. A large drawer made especially deep for liquor bottles slides out from one side of the cube.

Casual dining partners, such as the butcher block table and contemporary chairs shown here, make a family room a favorite place for informal meals or snacks. And when you choose lightweight chairs like these, they'll easily move in front of the television set or into your main seating area.

Also, consider lighting needs when you plan your family room. This is especially important if your room is in the basement or lacks windows. Creative illumination, like the grid of individual globe fixtures used in this setting, can make a room come alive with brightness and color.

TEMPLATES: DINING ROOM PIECES AND STORAGE UNITS

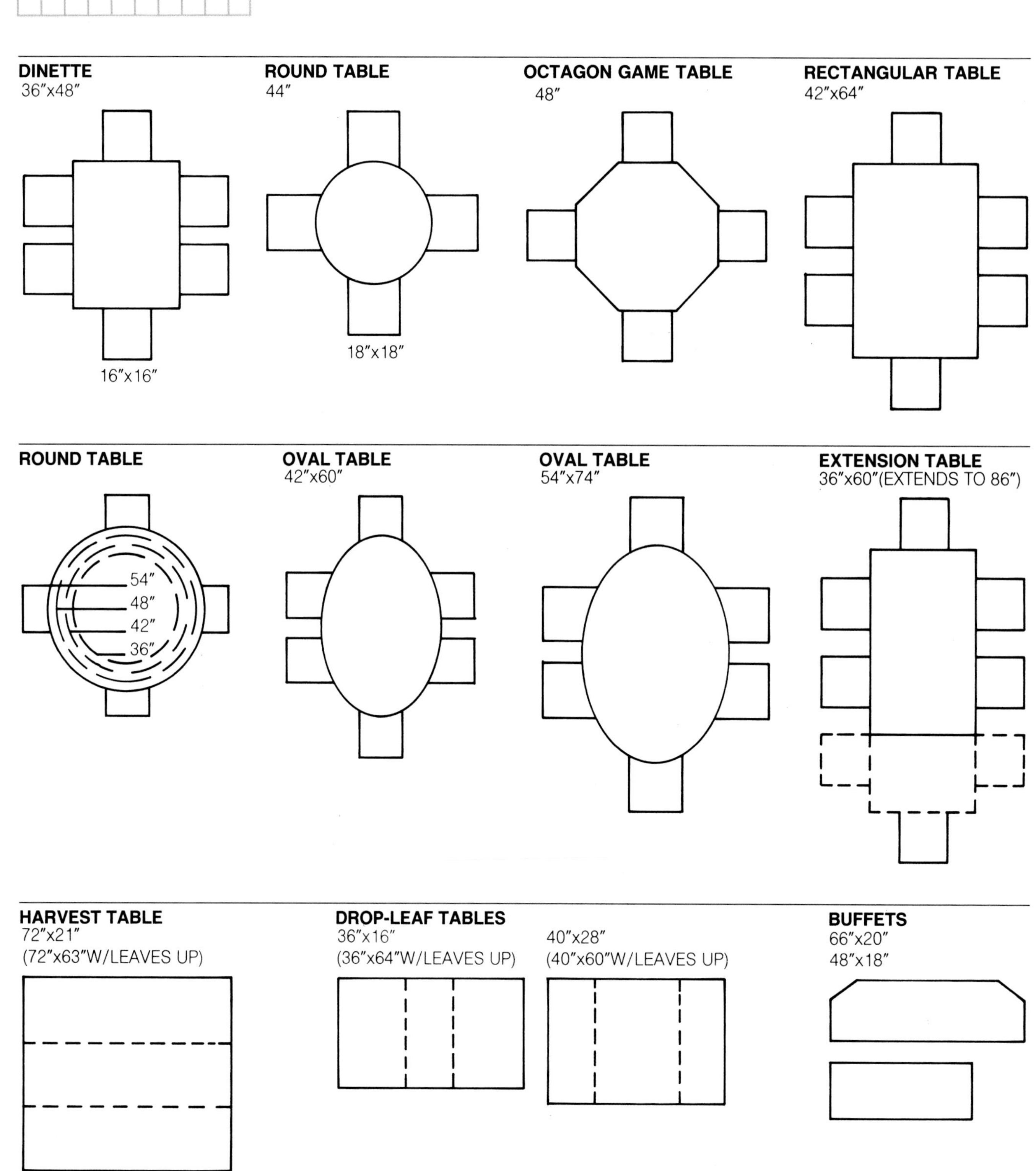

STORAGE UNITS

21"x30" 21"x36" 21"x40" 21"x44" 21"x48" 21"x60"

21"x64" 21"x68" 21"x78" 21"x84"

19"x19" 19"x30" 19"x33" 19"x36" 19"x38" 19"x42" 19"x45"

19"x48" 19"x52" 19"x60" 19"x66" 19"x72"

17"x25" 17"x30" 17"x36" 17"x38" 17"x42" 17"x48" 17"x52"

17"x60" 17"x66" 17"x72"

STACKING BOOKCASES

18"x36" EACH 11"x34" EACH

13"x36" 13"x44" 13"x48" 13"x52"

ARMOIRES

21"x38" 23"x41"

HALL CONSOLE

12"x42"

LINGERIE CHEST

14"x20"

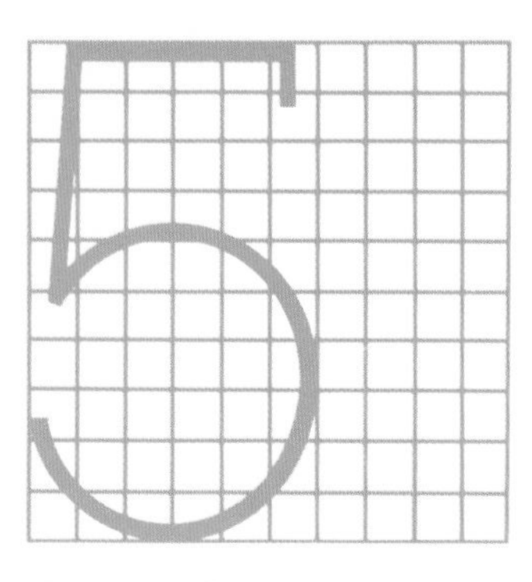

SHOPPING SENSE

The true beauty in a piece of high-quality furniture is considerably more than skin deep. What it's made of and how the components are put together have everything to do with how well—and how long—an item will serve your family's needs. This chapter gives you the information you need to buy wisely.

CASE GOODS

Shopping for case goods—unupholstered furniture pieces such as cabinets, chests, desks, étagères, wall units, headboards, and tables—isn't as complicated as it may seem. Once you know a few facts about construction and materials, you can judge the quality of a piece with a quick examination.

You'll be pleased to know, too, that good quality isn't limited to high-priced case goods. Many moderately priced wood furnishings offer long-lasting value and good design.

Survey your needs
As with any furniture purchase, it's best to evaluate your needs and wants *before* you shop. That way you'll simplify your shopping and be assured of buying furniture that will live up to your expectations. Here are some good questions to start with:

- *What needs will the piece serve?* Are you looking for a no-frills chest for extra sweaters, or an armoire that can serve as the focal point of your bedroom scheme?
- *Will the piece fit in the room?* Take careful measurements. Nothing is worse than bringing furniture home only to find out it's too large or small for the space you've reserved for it.
- *What furniture style complements your room setting?* Although mixing and matching furniture styles can give a room personality and charm, a new purchase should continue the basic mood you've already established.
- *How much can you spend?* Establish your budget at home, then stick to it when you shop.

(continued)

ASSESSING WOOD FURNITURE

A look at this list will tell you which wooden case goods are worth their price.

- Is the piece stable when you gently push down on a top corner or press your weight against the side?
- Are side, front, and back pieces joined with dovetail, mortise-and-tenon, tongue-and-groove, or double-dowel joints? (More about these on page 70.)
- Are corners on heavier pieces reinforced with corner blocks that are screwed *and* glued in place?
- Is the back panel inset and attached with screws?
- Do drawers and doors fit well and move smoothly?
- Are corners of drawers dovetailed?
- Are drawers snag-free?
- Do long shelves have center supports, and are any extensions sturdy?
- Are hinges strong and well secured?
- Do modular pieces fit together well? Does the finish on all the units match?
- Is the finish smooth, even, and consistent?
- Is the hardware secure?
- Does the hardware complement the furniture?
- Does the label identify the composition or construction of exposed surfaces?
- Is care advice included?
- Do larger pieces have casters?
- Are leveling mechanisms built in?

CASE GOODS

(continued)

Once you've pinpointed the kind of case piece you want, it's time to brush up on important construction points .

What to look for

The true test for almost any piece of furniture is how well it's put together. Using a few basic standards, you can tell easily how case goods rate.

Begin with the frame. It should be sturdy, strong, and made of solid, kiln-dried hardwood. Sometimes metal braces are added to further strengthen the frame.

Check the joints. The type used in building the frame largely determines how strong and stable the frame will be. Although you will be unable to see all the joints in a furniture piece, ask your furniture dealer what types are used.

- *Mortise-and-tenon joints* are the strongest and are used at major support points in good furniture. They consist of two sections, one with a square extension and the other with a square opening. Check the illustration *below* to see how they and other types of joints fit together.
- *Doweled joints* have round wooden pegs inserted into matching holes in the adjoining piece. Joints with three pegs are the strongest; single-dowel joints are the weakest; they can rotate and, in time, work their way loose.
- *Dovetail joints*—a sign of good-quality drawers in tables, chests, and kitchen cabinets—have notched wood that interlocks like a puzzle.
- *Rabbeted joints* are formed by cutting a rectangular groove along the surface of one piece so it interlocks with the edge of the opposite piece. They're used for drawer bottoms or supporting shelves.
- *Tongue-and-groove joints* consist of a continuous ridge that runs the full length of the board and fits into a recess along the edge of the adjoining piece.
- *Miter joints* are made of two pieces, each cut at an angle to form a corner.

To be strong, joints must be screwed and glued together. Nails or staples are not enough. For reinforcement, all major joints should have corner blocks that are screwed into place. Look for corner blocks at the juncture of table and chair legs and the frame, on the bottoms of drawer corners, and at the corners of chairs' seat frames.

The way drawers are constructed is a good indication of the overall quality of a piece. If your piece has no drawers, check a drawer of a companion piece by the same manufacturer. Good drawers feature dovetail joints, heavy-duty drawer guides, and smoothly finished insides. Corner blocks screwed into each corner on the underside will stabilize the drawer. Drawer bottoms should be held in rabbeted grooves, not stapled or nailed into place.

Also check the back and side panels of a piece. They, too, should be inserted into grooves, not simply held in place by nails or staples.

Feel the finish

Wooden case goods come with many different types of finishes, but regardless of the finish, a piece should have smooth, consistent, and attractive surfaces.

The finest furniture is hand finished. Because the hand-finishing process may involve as many as 20 time-consuming steps, the price for these pieces usually is much higher than for similar pieces that are machine finished.

A good way to learn about finishes is to look at both low- and high-priced furniture. Compare the hardness of finishes, their smoothness, color, and sheen or patina. Poorly finished pieces may have some finishing material visible in the crevices, or uneven streaks. A good finish is even in color, with a patina that comes with hand rubbing.

Feel all edges to be certain they're smooth and sanded. If the piece isn't going against a wall, the back should be finished as well as the front is.

Each type of finish has its advantages.

- *A painted or lacquered finish* is easy to clean but may be hard to touch up if scratched or dented.
- *Oil* is a good natural protector for wood, but you have to apply more oil every six months or so.

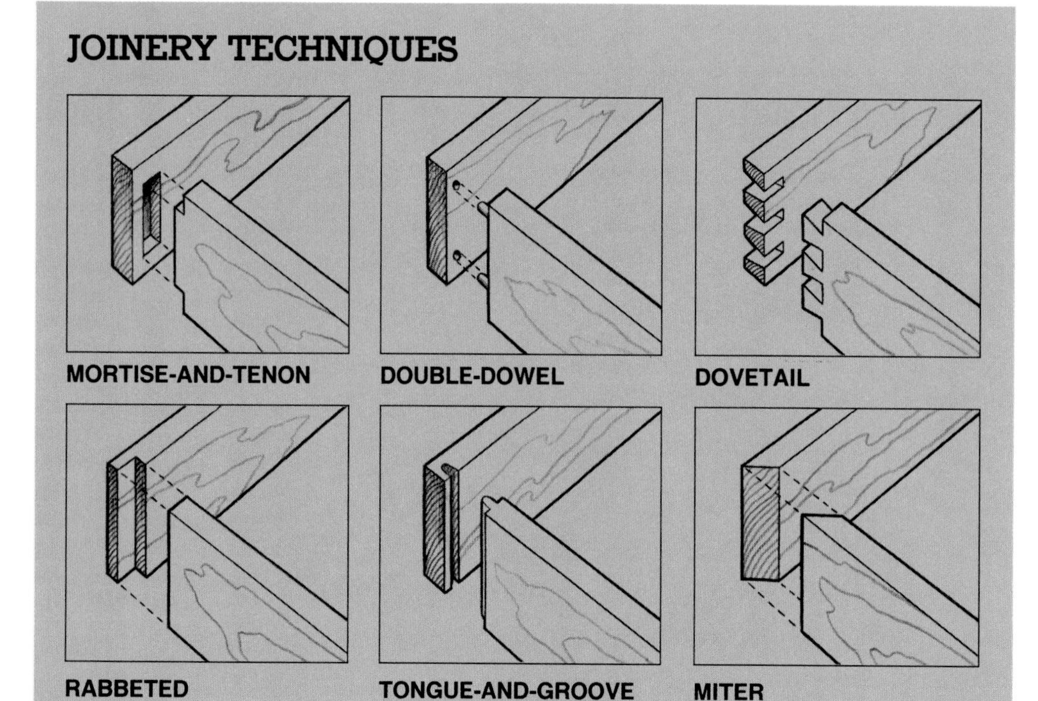

• *The "super-finishes,"* such as catalyzed *lacquers, synthetic varnishes, polyurethanes, epoxies, and vinyls,* are the most protective and durable.

Learn from the label

Many of today's furniture manufacturers provide helpful information about their products on hangtags and labels. Here's a rundown of some of the common terms used on labels and what they mean to you.

• *Solid* means that all exposed surfaces are made of lumber ¼ inch thick (or more) of the identified wood. Wood used in inner or hidden construction, however, can be of other types. Solid-wood surfaces don't necessarily make a furniture piece stronger or better, but they do make it cost more.

• *Genuine* means that all exposed surfaces and parts are of the wood indicated. Legs generally are solid wood; veneers may appear on top, sides, and fronts of drawers and doors.

• *All-wood construction* means that the exposed parts are all made of wood to the full thickness and extent of the panel. Some manufacturers skimp by gluing a thin layer of wood to a wood frame, giving it the appearance of thick wood from the outside. You can test this by simply thumping the panel. Thick wood construction gives a dead sound; a thin panel sounds hollow.

• *Veneer* is a composite of wood slices bonded in sandwich form. The center core is of a lightweight soft wood. Superimposed over and under this core are very thin sheets of stronger hardwood with grains running at right angles to those in the softwood core. Veneers resist warping and make dramatic graining effects possible.

• *Hardwoods,* which are preferred for high-quality case goods and upholstered furniture, come from deciduous trees. Popular hardwoods include cherry, oak, maple, walnut, mahogany, pecan, and birch.

• *Softwoods* are generally from evergreen trees and are more readily available and inexpensive than hardwoods. Adequately seasoned and kiln-dried pine can be satisfactory wood for furniture. However, unseasoned or poor-quality softwoods split and splinter easily.

Other terms on labels often are industry phrases. For instance, *"simulated wood components"* and *"wood-grained vinyl veneer"* describe plastic parts molded or painted to look like wood.

How about the hardware?

A thorough examination of case goods includes checking the hardware. Is it both functional and tastefully designed? Hardware should facilitate the opening and closing of movable parts, and its appearance should complement the piece, not overpower it.

Hardware on most lines of high-quality case goods is made of brass, although pewter, carved wood, or other materials also may be used. Brass-plated or painted hardware, used on lower-priced items, may not retain its good looks.

Handle the hardware. If it's metal, it will feel solid. Make sure that drawer pulls made of two connected parts—for example, handles fastened to a decorative back plate—are well secured.

CHROME- AND BRASS-PLATED FURNITURE

Many of today's case goods sparkle with chrome- or brass-plated finishes. These finishes are only skin deep, however, so it's important to know something about how they are applied and how to judge good-quality plated furniture.

In the plating process—known as *electroplating*—an electric current transfers a thin layer of chrome or brass to a highly polished steel surface. An extra step is involved in brass-plated furniture. Because brass oxidizes when left unprotected, the newly plated surface receives a coating of lacquer. This prevents tarnishing as long as the lacquer isn't penetrated. If a scratch in the protective layer exposes the underlying brass to air, oxidation and discoloration are apt to occur.

Chrome- and brass-plated furniture can have any one of several finishes:

• *A polished finish* is smooth and shiny.

• *A satin finish* has a grainy, brushed surface.

• Brass-plated pieces can be *"antiqued"* to resemble bronze.

How can you judge quality?

Generally, the cost of a chrome- or brass-plated furniture piece gives you your first clue about quality. Heavily plated pieces are costly. Meticulous details are also a sign of high quality.

• Before buying chrome- or brass-plated furniture, check the metal surfaces; they should be smooth and flat. Run your hand over the finish; if the metal feels rough, this means it has a grainy residue from the plating. Although some pitting of the finish is almost impossible to avoid, the indentations shouldn't be readily visible or detract from the appearance. The metal finish of less-expensive chrome furniture shows more irregularities and scratches.

• Check joints; they should be smooth and polished. Rough joints are signs of inferior quality. The joints may have a slightly different color from the rest of the piece; this variance is the result of a "jump" in the electric current during the plating process. Although some discoloration is unavoidable, especially in right-angle joints, good-quality chrome- or brass-plated furniture will have less color distortion than lower-quality furniture.

How do you care for plated furniture?

To maintain the luster of chrome-plated furniture, shine the surface with metal polish. Simply wipe brass-plated surfaces clean with a soft, dry cloth; new brass and brass-plated furniture almost always is lacquered, and metal polish may scratch the lacquer.

UPHOLSTERY

When you're shopping for upholstery, keep comfort foremost in mind. After all, what good is a chair or sofa if it doesn't sit well? While in the store, feel free to curl up or recline on any upholstered furniture you're considering. This is one kind of furniture you should "try on" before you buy.

Upholstery comes in so many different styles, shapes, and sizes that it's easy to become confused about just what to buy. Before you begin shopping, ask yourself a few questions.

• *What kind of seating do you need—a sofa, chair, love seat, recliner, or chaise?* Consider your seating needs as well as your space limitations. A sectional sofa, for example, provides more seating than two chairs in about the same amount of space. If you plan to move frequently, it's best to choose pieces that will work in a variety of rooms. A combination of sofa and love seat can be arranged in a number of ways, whereas an 80-inch sofa provides minimal flexibility.

• *Where will the piece go, and who will use it?* If your family room needs a chair that will become the favorite lounging spot for kids, consider durability and easy cleanability. A chair for a formal living room, on the other hand, can be much more delicate. Explain how you'll use a piece, and your furniture dealer can guide you toward a good selection.

• *What kind of upholstery is appropriate for your home?* Style is a personal preference, but it's good to periodically evaluate whether the style of your furnishings matches your life-style. If your family enjoys casual gatherings more than formal cocktail parties, seating pieces that have fussy fabrics and straight backs probably are not for you. You might want a silk-upholstered chaise in the master bedroom, but for family areas, it would be best to stick with easygoing pieces.

Once you've defined the type of upholstered piece you need, brush up on some upholstery construction basics. The information here and on the next two pages can help you understand what you're looking for; the shopping checklist *below* condenses the information into questions you can ask at the store.

Undercover concerns

Purchase upholstered furniture from the inside out. Although the cover fabric is important and can add a great deal to the overall appearance of a chair or sofa, it cannot make up for poor inner construction.

As with case goods, high-quality upholstered furniture construction starts with a sturdy frame. Most frames are made of kiln-dried hardwood, but some good-quality pieces use metal and high-impact polystyrene.

In the case of wood frames, check to see that they have screwed-in corner blocks where legs emerge from the corners. Rear legs that are an extension of the frame provide the greatest stability. Legs screwed onto a metal plate on the seat frame will begin to wobble in time; avoid furniture with this feature. All frame joints should be glued and double-doweled to provide sturdiness. *(continued)*

ASSESSING UPHOLSTERY

Ask these questions about the upholstered items you look at.

• What is the frame made of? (Hardwood is the industry standard, but some good-quality pieces have metal or high-impact polystyrene frames.)
• Are double-doweled joints used to join the parts of the frame?
• Are corners reinforced with corner blocks?
• Are legs solid extensions of the frame or attached securely to the frame and braced with corner blocks?
• Does the spring system offer resilient, soft support?
• Are springs covered with burlap to separate them from the cushioning materials?
• Is thick padding used so you can't feel the frame underneath?
• Does the fabric hold its shape when you stretch a sample of it in all directions?
• Is the fabric stain- and soil-resistant?
• Will the fabric resist snagging?
• Is the cover well sewn? (Check for straight seams, matched patterns, secure buttons, and a lined skirt.)
• When you sit in the upholstered piece, are the seat, arm, and back heights comfortable?
• Are the back and seat soft yet resilient?
• Are the materials used to make the cover, cushioning, and frame identified?
• Are the fabric and, in sleep sofas and recliners, metal mechanisms covered by warranties?
• Is care advice included?

NEW YORK

UPHOLSTERY

(continued)

Connected to an upholstery frame is the *base* or *spring support.* This usually is a webbing made of closely interwoven jute or polypropylene strips and reinforced with metal strips. The webbing should have no open spaces in it; any gaps could weaken the support.

Spring systems
You'll find two main types of springs used in upholstery—*sagless* and *coil.* Both types, illustrated *below,* should be made of tempered steel.

- *Sagless springs* are flat, wavy lines of high-grade steel and are used most often in lightly scaled contemporary lines. Sagless springs should be used with *helical springs,* as illustrated *below*, to give them greater strength and stability. They produce what is called a "rigid-edge seat" that is tighter and less resilient than the "spring-edge seat."
- *Coil springs* produce a resilient, comfortable seat often referred to as a "spring-edge seat." Twelve coil springs per seat or cushion provide a good base. When seven or fewer are used, the spaces between the springs become too large to provide even support.

In coil construction, each spring is tied at right angles in two directions and diagonally, resulting in eight knots on each spring. This is why the phrase "hand-tied eight ways" denotes fine-quality construction. Some manufacturers have cut labor costs by reducing the number of ties to six.

The main differences between the two types of spring systems are comfort and price; the extra labor and time needed to tie coil springs increase the cost of an upholstered piece. Both coil springs and sagless springs are durable if properly installed. Which you find more comfortable is largely a matter of personal choice.

- Some upholstered pieces have *fabric slings* in place of springs to support the cushions. This cuts cost, but it also diminishes comfort and durability.

Padding possibilities
Upholstery padding can be any of a variety of materials.

- *Down,* once widely used as a filling, is now too expensive for most furniture pieces.
- *Latex foam (foam rubber)* and *polyurethane foam (polyfoam)* are the two most widely used padding materials for upholstery.

Latex foam cushions are comfortable and can be molded into special shapes. Many people consider foam rubber to be the most resilient cushioning material, but it does dry and pulverize after extended use. Also, solvent-base cleaning agents can cause it to disintegrate.

Polyurethane foam is strong, does not crust or shed, is unaffected by solvent cleaners, and is less expensive than latex foam. Fabric doesn't slide over polyurethane, so it's easy to keep welts and seams straight and in place.

Good-quality furniture cushions have a latex or polyfoam core with a layer of man-made fiber batting over it for comfort and a softer contour. Look for Dacron polyester batting, which is nonallergenic and not damaged by insects, solvents, or alcohol. Rubberized hair is commonly used in medium-priced furniture, and it's acceptable. Avoid battings made of moss, tow, excelsior, kapok, or sisal; they aren't durable.

Facts about fabrics
Fabric selection is the most enjoyable part of buying upholstered furniture, but remember

HOW CHAIRS ARE CONSTRUCTED

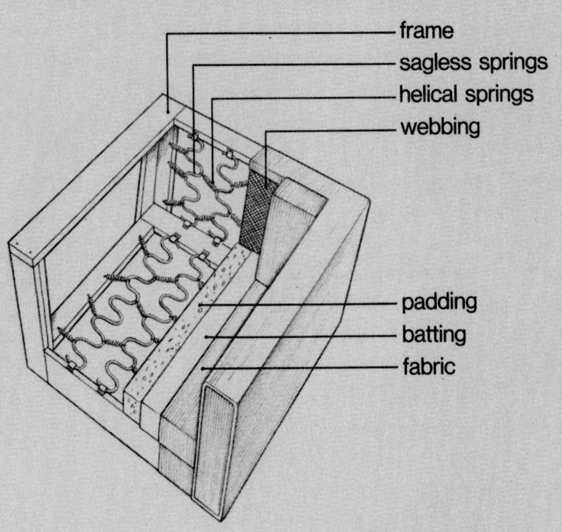

SAGLESS SPRINGS

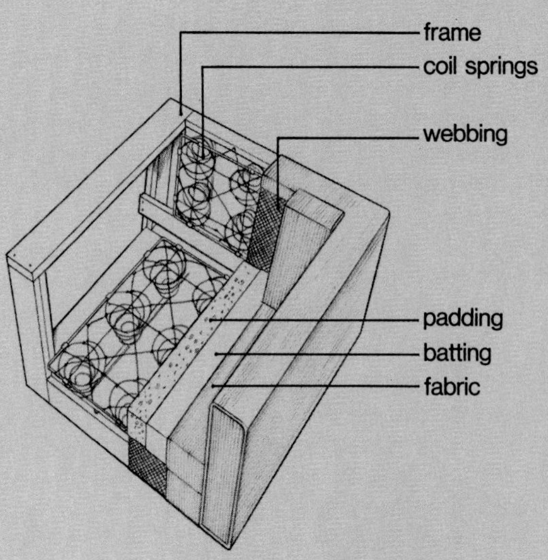

COIL SPRINGS

to consider durability as well as appearance. The high cost of reupholstering makes the first fabric choice you make especially important.

A fabric's fiber content can tell you a great deal about how the fabric will perform. If the label doesn't list the fabric information, ask for it. Often, manufacturers blend fibers in upholstery fabrics to take advantage of the good qualities of several fibers. Natural materials—such as wool, cotton, silk, and linen, for instance—lend a good feel, or "hand," to fabrics. They also dye well. Synthetic fibers—such as polyester and nylon—on the other hand, provide extra strength and durability. The fibers present in the greatest percentages determine most of the fabric's characteristics.

You can get a pretty good idea of a fabric's potential by evaluating the characteristics listed here according to fibers:

- *Wool* offers very good abrasion resistance, dyes well, and is easy to clean. It can feel scratchy or rough, however, depending on the weave and the yarn.
- *Cotton* dyes beautifully, but is not as strong as wool. To be soil resistant, it needs treating.
- *Silk* offers luxurious feel and wide color choices, but has poor resistance to abrasion and soil.
- *Linen* resists abrasion, but wrinkles easily. Dyed linen also tends to lose its color in areas of heavy abrasion, such as arms and seats.
- *Acetate* offers only fair resistance to abrasion and needs treatment for soil resistance; it dyes fairly well.
- *Acrylic, nylon,* and *olefin (polypropylene)* all resist abrasion and are easy to clean.
- *Polyester* isn't as strong as acrylic, nylon, or olefin, but it is easy to clean if treated to repel oil, and it resists wrinkles.
- *Rayon* offers fair abrasion resistance and needs treatment with a soil repellent.

In addition to fiber content, evaluate a fabric's construction or weave. Fabrics with tight, close weaves wear longer than those with loose weaves. Hold samples toward a light source to compare thickness and consistency. Stretch the fabric on the crosswise and lengthwise grain lines to check for possible shifting of threads.

Ask about chemically applied finishes that resist stains. Some fabrics need no additional stain repellents. Olefin, for example, is naturally stain resistant. Some finishes resist both water and oil stains; some resist only water-based stains.

Most manufacturers grade their upholstery fabrics with a numerical or alphabetical system. It's important to remember that these grades are related to the cost of a fabric and don't necessarily reflect the fabric's durability. An intricate brocade, for instance, is an expensive fabric to produce and therefore is a high-grade selection. Brocade, however, doesn't wear as well as a tightly woven cotton fabric of a lower grade.

If you can't find a sofa or chair in the fabric you like on the showroom floor, ask whether other upholstery pattern and color choices are available. Some retailers stock an inventory of upholstered pieces, but more often than not you will have to custom-order to get exactly what you want. Special ordering may cost more than buying off the floor, and you'll have to wait several weeks for home delivery, but you'll get what you really want in the end.

ASSESSING FOAM FURNITURE

Since its introduction in the 1960s, foam furniture has soared in popularity—thanks to contemporary looks, modest price tags, easy care, and flexibility. But, as with conventional frame pieces, it's important to judge the quality of foam furnishings from the inside out. Here are some things to consider before you buy.

What kind of foam furniture is available?
Foam furniture is made in a wide variety of styles, shapes, and sizes. Some pieces are simply blocks and slabs of foam joined to form seats with low backs; others have shaped arms and backs for a more conventional look. Many convert to twin-, double-, or queen-size beds. And modular foam pieces can go together in a number of configurations.

Covers for foam furnishings also vary. Nylon parachute cloth in fashion colors is a popular, durable cover, but most high-quality lines also include cotton prints or solids and wool blends.

How is foam furniture made?
High-quality pieces are made of layers of different-density foam that are laminated or glued together. The highest-density foam is used for the framework of the back, arms, and base, and provides resilient support. Softer foam makes up the cushiony, outer layers.

Low-quality furniture made of solid blocks of low-density foam usually looks good when new but soon sags and loses its shape. Although most pieces are 100 percent polyurethane foam (check the label), some low-end pieces are made of "loaded foam" that contains clay or other minerals. These fillers artificially increase the foam's density and weight, and also cause the foam to pack down and deteriorate. If you suspect a sofa or chair is made of loaded foam, pick the piece up. If it's heavy and low-priced, you're probably right.

How to judge quality?
It's almost impossible to determine the quality of foam pieces by sight alone, but you can test it several other ways. First check the hangtag or label for the foam's density. If the information isn't listed, ask a salesperson to check the manufacturer's catalog. The best foam for seating units is 1.5 weight, meaning a 12-inch cube weighs 1.5 pounds.

Before buying a foam piece, try it out, as you would any other type of furniture. Sit down, lean back, stretch out—if the piece gives too much under your weight, the foam isn't dense enough to provide lasting comfort. Push down on the arms and back. They should feel solid yet resilient. If the piece is a sleeper, unfold the bed and lie down. The sleeping surface should provide firm, uniform support.

MATTRESSES

Although it's not a piece of furniture per se, your mattress is one of the most important home furnishings you purchase. A good mattress will provide 10 to 15 years of sleeping comfort. At eight hours a night, that's at least 29,000 hours of faithful service—quite a payoff for a couple of hours of careful shopping.

Most conventional mattresses look basically the same on the outside, but inside they have a wealth of difference in their quality, construction, comfort, and prices. Because sleeping comfort is a matter of personal preference, there's no such thing as the universal "perfect" mattress. To help pinpoint what you want from a mattress, ask these questions.

- *Who will use the mattress?* Take physical characteristics, such as weight and height, into consideration. A tall person may need an extra-long mattress, for instance.
- *What are your sleeping habits?* Do you stretch out at night, or do you naturally occupy only a small part of the mattress? This is an especially important factor when two people share a mattress. Besides providing ample sleep space, the mattress has to meet differing comfort standards.
- *How will you use the mattress?* Do you need a mattress that doubles as seating? If so, look for features that will help ensure durability.

Try out store samples
The only way to tell whether a mattress is right for you is to test it. Lie down on it for at least 10 minutes (almost any mattress will feel comfortable at first.) Stretch, bounce, and roll around, just as you would when sleeping. If two share the mattress, test it together.

The mattress should support areas of greatest weight, such as the shoulders and hips. The support should be firm, but resilient to ensure comfort.

Mattress edges are another indicator of quality. A good mattress has reinforced sides to prevent sagging when you sit on the edge of the bed. The edge may give under your weight, but it should spring back when you stand up.

When you shop, ask what's under the cover. If the salesperson can't tell you, ask to see a catalog or brochure from the manufacturer. Also, look at a cutaway model, if one is available. (More about mattress construction on pages 78 and 79.)

Always read the attached hangtag and label, which provide information about the materials and construction.

"Firm" for whom?
Although many doctors recommend hard mattresses—or even semihard ones—for patients with back problems, they are not for everyone. Also, manufacturers' definitions of firmness may vary, so don't rely on labels such as "extra-firm" or "ultra-firm." Determine for yourself whether the mattress is comfortable.

If you know that you want firmness, a conventional innerspring mattress with thick-wired coils and extra-strong perimeter wires may be a good choice. A box spring with a built-in backboard also will increase the firmness.

Or, select an innerspring mattress that has firm support and is cushioned by an extra-plush top. These soft-top mattresses usually are the highest quality and highest priced models in a line. The extra cushioning layers make these mattresses 2 or 3 inches thicker than standard types of mattresses. *(continued)*

MATTRESS SIZES

Which bed size you need depends on your size, whether you sleep alone or with someone, and how much room you want. These standard mattress sizes are generally recognized by manufacturers, but measurements can vary slightly. As a rule, a mattress should be at least 6 inches longer than the person sleeping on it. If you're buying a bed for two adults, consider a queen- or king-size bed. A full-size bed offers each person only the sleeping space of a crib.

NAME	SIZE (in inches)
Single or Youth	75x30-34
Twin Regular	75x38
Twin Extra-Long	80x38
Full Regular	75x53
Full Extra-Long	80x53
Queen Regular	80x60
Queen Extra-Long	84x60
King Regular	80x76
King Extra-Long	84x76
Eastern King	80x78
California King	84x72

twin
full
queen
king

STANDARD MATTRESS SIZES

MATTRESSES

(continued)

The most widely used types of conventional mattresses are *innerspring* and *foam* mattresses. Innerspring mattresses, which provide highly resilient and often durable sleeping surfaces, have steel coils sandwiched between layers of insulation and cushioning material. Foam mattresses generally are made of polyurethane and can be soft, moderately firm, or firm, depending on the density of the foam.

The inner workings of an innerspring mattress
Although many people think the number of coils in an innerspring mattress is an indication of its quality, the thickness of the coil wire, the number of coil convolutions, and the way the coils work together to support your body count far more. Generally, the thicker the wire and the more convolutions, the firmer the support. High-quality models usually have coils made of low-gauge (thick) wire with six turns. Coils in medium-priced and lower-priced mattresses are thinner and have fewer convolutions.

The springs have an insulator covering—a tough fiber padding, wire, or netting, or a combination of the three—that separates the mattress cushioning from the coils.

Mattresses usually are cushioned with polyurethane foam, combined with cotton felt or other fibers. The material is secured to the springs to keep it in place. Generous cushioning indicates high quality.

It's best to buy a matching box spring when you purchase a new innerspring mattress. The box spring will reinforce the support where needed and extend the life of the mattress. Like mattresses, box springs also have different coil counts, and the coils themselves may be cone- or hourglass-shape. Some foundations use metal grids or zigzag-shape torsion bars instead of coils. Box springs cost about the same as mattresses.

Some foundations are combinations of wood and foam, and do not use a spring system. Be sure that the foam layer in this type of foundation is at least a couple of inches thick for satisfactory support.

Weigh the facts on foam
The most expensive foam mattresses usually are made of latex rubber. The rubber is molded into a slab while in the liquid state and allowed to harden into a densely constructed foam core. Because of its scarcity and high cost, you'll find latex rubber in only a limited number of premium-quality mattresses.

Most foam mattresses are made of polyurethane, which is manufactured in large slabs and cut to size. Mattresses consisting of high-resilience polyurethane or polyurethane with embedded thermoplastic beads give optimum support and performance. Good-quality foam has a high density, which adds weight. A mattress made of very lightweight foam usually offers less than the greatest comfort.

It's important to check how a foam mattress is finished. Some manufacturers provide a layer of foam wrapped around the outside rim of the mattress to reduce spreading and sagging of the solid-core form. An edging of covered tape should hold this layer firmly in place. Tape also should secure the ticking.

Avoid foam pads that are loosely covered or wrapped. Improperly secured ticking on foam bases will creep and twist, and you'll eventually end up with a warped mattress. Tops and borders should have defined, piped edges. Look for air vents, too—they prevent build up of moisture and odor. Even with vents, however, foam mattresses may hold moisture when used in extremely humid climates. They are, however, nonallergenic and resist insects and mildew.

Ask about warranties
Manufacturers usually warrant high-quality mattresses and foundations against defective workmanship. For premium bedding, a 15-year warranty is common. Lower-quality bedding may be warranted for a shorter time.

Keep in mind that a warranty ensures workmanship; it does not guarantee that the mattress will provide optimum support and comfort for the total period of time stated.

Caring for your mattress
To prolong the life of a new innerspring mattress, turn it from side to side and head to foot each month for the first half-year, and then once every six months after that. This turning airs the mattress and helps keep it from sagging. Unlike innerspring mattresses, foam types don't need to be turned.

For best wear, a mattress needs more support than just that supplied by the foundation designed to accompany it; a sturdy bed frame also should support the entire system. The large mattresses, particularly the king-size, require extra center support rails.

ASSESSING INNERSPRING MATTRESSES

Here's what you need to ask yourself before you buy an innerspring mattress.

- Are the coils heavy gauge? More important than the number of coils is their thickness and the number of convolutions. Generally, the thicker the wire and the more turns, the firmer the support. High-quality models usually have coils made of heavy-gauge wire with six turns.
- Is the cushioning generous?
- Is the fabric durable, well sewn, and quilted to prevent bunching? (Top-of-the-line mattresses are covered with damask.)
- Are mattress edges reinforced to prevent sagging?
- Is the box spring matched to the mattress? (Box springs and mattresses perform best when used as sets.)
- Does the mattress give firm support to your hips, shoulders, and spine when you lie on it? (If two people will be using the mattress, they should test it together.)
- Is it big enough? (A mattress should be at least 6 inches longer than your height and provide ample sleeping space.)
- Are materials and construction data included?
- Is care advice listed?
- Is the warranty attached? (Most good-quality mattresses and foundations are warranted against defective workmanship for 10 to 15 years.)

IS A WATER BED FOR YOU?

For many people, "getting a good night's rest" means sleeping on a water bed. The flotation system distributes body weight evenly so tossing and turning are minimized. And the heated mattress is a comfort on cold nights. Interested? Read on.

Standard water-bed basics
A standard water bed consists of a water mattress, a heater, a frame with a safety liner, and a supportive deck and pedestal, as illustrated *at right.*

• When comparing water mattresses, check the quality of the materials and construction. All mattresses are made of vinyl (polyvinyl chloride), but the gauge of the vinyl differs among brands. Vinyl that's about 20 mils thick is usually adequate, but heavier vinyl sometimes is used.

The least expensive type of water mattress looks like a pillow made of two panels of vinyl that are joined on all four sides. In lower quality mattresses of this type, the pieces are equal in size and the seams fall along the edges. In better quality models, one large panel makes up both the top and the sides and joins another panel at the bottom. The seams are beneath the mattress, where stress is less.

Higher priced mattresses usually have top and bottom panels joined to side pieces. These box-shaped examples generally are stronger than pillow types.

The kind of seams a mattress has also indicates its quality. Butt seams, in which pieces join edge to edge, often are found on economy water mattresses. High-quality mattresses have double-sealed lap seams, which are more durable than butt seams.

• A water bed's heater is basically a flat waterproof heating pad that fits below the mattress and liner. Although some water beds come with factory-installed heating systems, most have separate heaters. Always check the heater for the Underwriters Laboratories (UL) label, an assurance of safe electrical components.

The major difference between heaters is the type of control used. Less expensive heaters usually have mechanical controls. Heaters made with solid-state controls cost more, but provide more precise temperature control.

• Every standard water bed should have a tough vinyl safety liner that catches any water that might leak out while you're filling or draining the mattress, or if the mattress is punctured. The best liners fit snugly inside the frame and are secured with plastic strips and screws.

• The frame, a bottomless box that surrounds a standard water-bed mattress, takes the pressure off the mattress.

• The deck, the platform a standard water mattress rests on, attaches to the frame with screws or brackets.

• You'll also need a sturdy pedestal, basically a recessed base, to raise a standard water bed to a comfortable height. A good pedestal has crosspieces that provide support beneath the entire bed.

Standard water mattresses come in conventional twin-, full-, queen-, and king-size widths, but are usually 7 feet long and 9 to 10 inches thick. These mattresses require special linens.

Although a large standard water bed can weigh around 2,000 pounds, the weight per square foot is generally less than that of a refrigerator. Any floor that meets modern standard building codes should support your water bed.

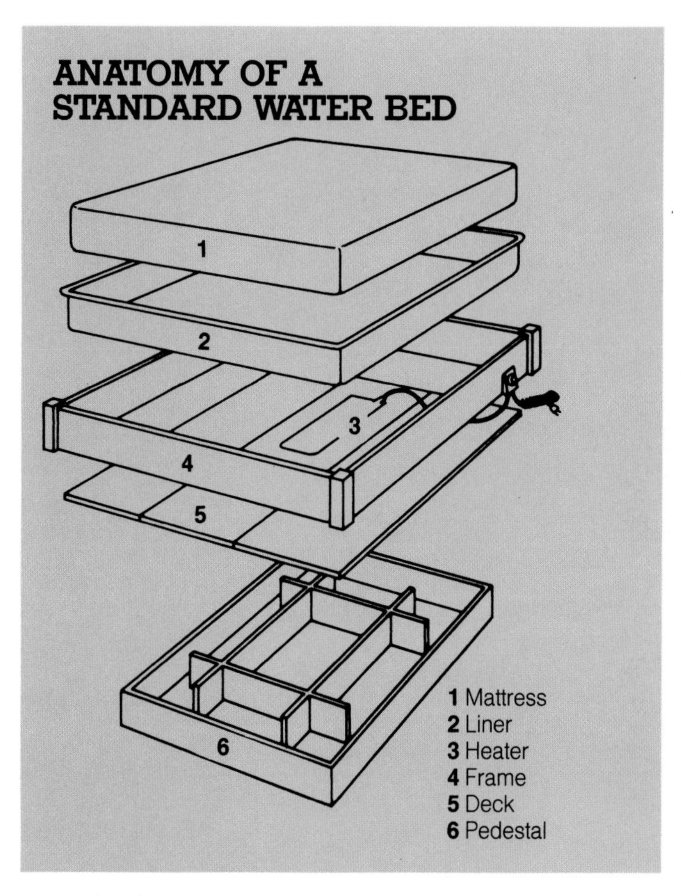

Consider a hybrid water bed
Hybrid water mattresses, which contain water-filled cavities surrounded by foam shells, are more expensive than standard water mattresses. They require half as much water and thus weigh much less than regular water beds. Because they're available in standard bed sizes, they often work well with conventional box springs. Also, they use conventional bed linens.

The water cavity of a hybrid water bed is constructed like a standard water mattress, so check for the same quality points. Also make sure the foam covering over the cavity is less than an inch thick; a heavier layer will inhibit the mattress' floating sensation.

Water mattresses without waves
Waveless mattresses provide the supportive buoyancy of regular water mattresses but have less motion. Baffles inside the mattresses restrict the side-to-side motion of the water and shorten the duration of up-and-down movement. Waveless mattresses are available in both standard and hybrid water-bed systems.

SECONDHAND AND UNFINISHED FURNITURE

When you're looking for good decorating value, be sure not to sell secondhand and unfinished furniture short. Both often offer sound quality at prices below the market norm for new, fully finished pieces. Secondhand and unfinished items help you add individual touches to your home, too. A turn-of-the-century table or a new desk stained to complement your den's color scheme can look considerably better than their cost would indicate.

There's no shortage of secondhand furniture, but it takes some shrewd shopping to find the best pieces. Here's a listing of sources that regularly produce worthy examples.

- *Auctions and estate sales.* In most cases, a bill of goods or a listing of the merchandise for sale accompanies newspaper advertisements for these events. Arrive early, if possible, so you can inspect the pieces.
- *House and garage sales.* You may find real bargains here, because vendors aren't necessarily out to make a huge profit. Usually the objective is to clear out household clutter. But one home's clutter is another's treasure; many homeowners—unwittingly or otherwise—price their merchandise far below market value. Again, watch the newspaper for listings of garage sales and go early to beat the crowd (unless advertisements specify "no early birds").
- *Consignment and thrift shops.* Outlets such as Salvation Army and Goodwill stores regularly offer a variety of used furniture. Most towns also have privately owned shops that specialize in secondhand pieces. Check the newspaper and the Yellow Pages for advertisements.
- *Special classified ad sections.* Listings in regular newspapers or weekly shoppers also are excellent hunting grounds for secondhand furniture. They often are specific, so you can zero in on the items that interest you. Then move fast—before the competition does.

Check quality first, price second

If a piece of furniture was well constructed and has had good care, it will probably be a good value when you buy it secondhand. But, to be safe, put every prospective purchase through these tests:

- Tables and chairs should be sturdy, not wobbly. Check how the legs are attached. Are there braces in corners and stretchers between chair legs?
- Check chests or pieces with drawers by pulling out a drawer and inspecting its construction. Are sides dovetailed? Are they varnished, but not painted? Unfinished wood will stick; painted wood may bind the drawer's movement.
- Hardware should be attached with screws and bolts that go all the way through to the back side of the piece.

The unfinished story

Once, unfinished furniture had very little to offer in the way of variety. Most pieces were made of medium- to low-quality pine, usually decked out with brass-plated "colonial" hardware.

Recently, however, the picture has changed dramatically. Now, unfinished furniture is available in virtually every style, price range, and quality level. And it's no longer limited to lumber and paint stores; look for unfinished items in any store that sells furniture. Some outlets even specialize in unfinished pieces.

Most major mail-order catalogs offer a number of unfinished pieces, as do many specialty mail-order companies. Some even offer high-quality reproductions of museum furniture.

Today's selections include basic, unadorned pieces; contemporary, dual-purpose furniture; and special items such as rolltop desks and four-poster beds. Styles range from Early American to Colonial, Victorian, Shaker, French, and contemporary. Many simple-lined unfinished pieces lend themselves to customizing, with a wide variety of hardware and finishes to choose from.

Quality guidelines

The type of wood used and the thoroughness of workmanship determine the quality of unfinished furniture.

- *Lower-priced pieces* usually are made of clear, soft white pine. This wood has little graining to add interest, so it looks best when painted, lacquered, or given an antique finish. Low-end pieces have bottoms and sides of fiberboard, with frames that are nailed together. Drawers generally are put together with staples.
- *Medium-quality furniture* often is made of knotty pine, which is tougher and harder than white pine. The knots add a rustic touch to the finished pieces. Other good-quality unfinished furniture pieces are made of maple, birch, and aspen. Maple has a rich, grained look and takes a warm, mellow finish. Construction is solid but without the extra touches that you'll find in top-of-the-line pieces.
- *Luxury pieces* are made of cherry and solid oak. When finished with care, these pieces look as elegant as a factory-finished piece—and you can choose the finish you want. Top-quality hardwood furniture often features the construction details that you see in fine finished pieces. The frames are sturdy, with corner blocks. Sides, doors, and drawers are made of wood, and drawers have center guides and dovetail joints. Additionally, the doors hang true on their hinges.

KIT FURNITURE

Kit furniture takes do-it-yourself decorating several steps beyond unfinished furniture: Everything you need to put together a piece of furniture is included in the kit, from wood to tools to varnish. Kit furniture offers several benefits: It usually costs 30 to 60 percent less than comparable finished pieces; because manufacturers can't hide the basic materials behind paint or upholstery, they're not likely to use inferior woods or take construction short-cuts; and the pride of putting together your own handsome Windsor chair or graceful Queen Anne dresser from a kit adds even more to its value to you.

The kit-furniture industry has grown tremendously in recent years. Whether you prefer traditional styles such as Queen Anne or Victorian, or lean toward a more contemporary look, there's a kit for you—probably more than one, in fact. Besides chairs and tables, you can get kits for desks, candlestands, rockers, armoires, beds, dressers, wall units, plant holders, benches, mirrors, hutches, and even clocks and musical instruments.

Many pieces are reproductions of Colonial or Shaker furniture. Others are adaptations inspired by past styles. (For more about antiques and reproductions, see pages 84-91.)

The companies that make furniture kits range from large and well established to tiny. Some of the larger firms run their own retail stores as well as offering mail-order catalogs. The smaller businesses are often home-based family-run enterprises that produce one or two kits. Although retail stores sell some furniture kits, specialty mail-order catalogs are the main sources.

Judging kit quality

Usually, the price of a kit is a good indicator of its quality. Since they have no easy ways to hide imperfections in unfinished, unassembled furniture, most manufacturers charge a fair price for the quality they provide.

Companies that use desirable hardwoods such as cherry, mahogany, or black walnut usually use the top grades of wood. A kit made of pine, however, may be either clear pine or a lower grade of knotty pine. Check the description to be sure. If you're buying a pine piece, it's also good to examine the parts that will sustain the most pressure, such as chair and table legs. These components should be made of a stronger wood, such as maple.

As with conventional furniture, look for dovetail or mortise-and-tenon joints to indicate sturdiness.

What's in a kit?

You'll get the component pieces, instructions, hardware, and—usually—glue, sandpaper, stain, and varnish. Be sure to check, however; sometimes the stain and finishing components are not furnished.

You'll need only a few tools; a screwdriver and a hammer usually are all that's required. If you are working on contemporary-style furniture, you also may use an Allen wrench (usually included in the package).

When you receive your kit, open it up and check the contents against the list provided by the manufacturer. Also check the wood for any dents or nicks. Take care of minor indentations by simply applying a little water to the area. The wood should swell and the dent disappear.

ORDERING FURNITURE BY MAIL

Ordering furniture of any kind through the mail can save you time and money. But, because you can't examine the goods firsthand, it's important to keep several pointers in mind.

- Buy from a company with an established reputation. If you're unfamiliar with a firm, check with the Better Business Bureau or local consumer protection office.
- Before ordering, read the product description carefully for key information. Don't rely on a photograph. Some catalogs state that a comparable substitute will be sent if what you ordered is unavailable. If you don't want a substitute, clearly say so on your order.
- Before you buy, find out whether the merchandise you want is offered on a "satisfaction-guaranteed" or "money-back" basis. If the company's refund policy is unclear, ask for clarification.
- Check warranty terms, especially if you're purchasing major items. Find out what recourse you have if the kit doesn't live up to the manufacturer's specifications.
- If you plan to pay in installments, study the credit plan to find out exactly how much you will pay, and when.
- Keep a record of your order, including the name and address of the company and the date you placed the order. Also, make note of the date your order is to be delivered by.
- Send a personal check, money order, or major credit card number instead of cash. Include shipping and handling charges and applicable sales taxes.

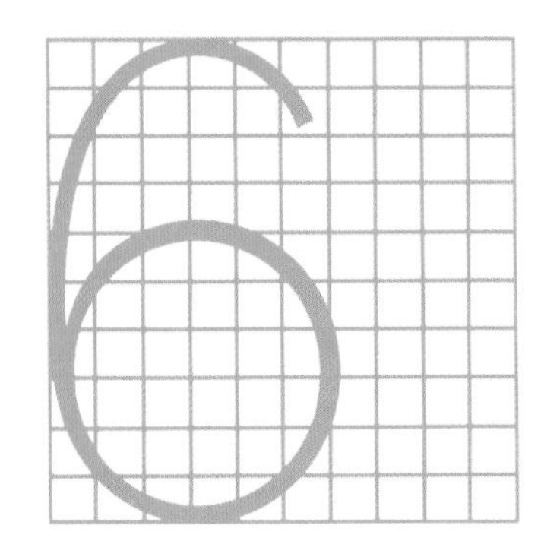

USING YESTERDAY'S FURNITURE TODAY

ANTIQUES, REPRODUCTIONS, ADAPTATIONS, & HANDCRAFTED FURNITURE

Looking for furniture you can be pretty sure you won't see in someone else's home? This chapter tells about what could be called "limited editions"—antiques (and items that will be antiques in the not-too-distant future), modern-day reproductions and adaptations of antique pieces, and distinctive furniture made by individual artisans. Here's how to distinguish antiques from plain old furniture, and good plain old furniture from junk. You'll also learn what to look for when shopping for reproductions or adaptations, and where to seek out handcrafted pieces that just might become tomorrow's heirlooms.

Doing the unexpected can add excitement to life, and the same holds true for the way you decorate your home. The most interesting rooms often veer from the tried and true to achieve something different.

The living room shown *at left* is a pleasingly eclectic case in point. Here a contemporary sofa and love seat and a custom-made, geometric-patterned rug are right at home in a house that is itself a turn-of-the-century charmer. A glass-topped center table combines old-time motifs with twentieth-century workmanship. And most of the other furnishings are either genuine antiques (in the United States this means at least 100 years old) or just plain old.

The old-timers have varied backgrounds: The stately armoire came from France, the intricately trimmed corner table (originally a flower cart) from England, and the twig chair is an example of American primitive craftsmanship. That they get along so well together proves that doing the unexpected can be as rewarding in decorating as in anything else. This room also shows how well yesterday's furnishings work in today's homes.

When mixing contemporary and antique furnishings, strive to develop a unifying theme. Color offers one of the basic keys to unity. Choose one color or a few basic colors to connect pieces of varying moods and vintages. Here, accents of crimson and navy appear throughout the room in the form of toss pillows, lampshades, and seat cushions. The area rug picks up these colors, adds a few of its own, and serves as a focal point that defines the conversation area. *(continued)*

USING YESTERDAY'S FURNITURE TODAY

(continued)

Many people shy away from owning antiques or good pieces of almost-antique furniture for fear that the pieces won't "fit" or make practical sense in their surroundings. If you're one of these people, here are some thoughts to consider.

First, keep in mind that although fine old furniture is meant to be cherished, it's also meant to be lived with comfortably. Except perhaps for certain museum-quality pieces, most of yesterday's furniture can function as originally intended, or easily be adapted or converted for new purposes and decorative uses. (To learn about caring for antiques, see page 94.)

Most antiques live quite well outside their period setting. One of the most effective ways to play up the presence of a beautiful old piece is to let it stand alone in an otherwise contemporary setting. For example, the dining room pictured *at left,* with its antique display shelf and its smooth, marble-slab table, shows just how striking this old/new juxtaposition can be. Another decorative counterpoint comes from the no-nonsense industrial light fixture—hardly the kind of "chandelier" you'd expect to find in an architecturally traditional room like this one.

The large pine cabinet in the entryway pictured *below* works well in a more traditional but still highly functional setting. More than just an announcement of the homeowners' interest in antiques, the cabinet is perfect for holding keys and mail and for storing seasonal items such as scarves, gloves, and boots.

Not all that glitters

Bear in mind, too, that not all antiques are *fine* antiques, and that not all old furniture will ripen into golden age on its 100th birthday. Many pieces are simply old—sometimes even poorly designed. If you have a piece that's truly homely, or in such poor condition that it's not worth preserving as is, by all means paint or restyle it to meet your own needs. Just make sure that the item you're dealing with is not valuable—from a historical, aesthetic, or economic point of view—before you make any changes; once antiques lose their original features, they lose much of their intrinsic value.

FURNISHING WITH REPRODUCTIONS AND ADAPTATIONS

Fine, authentic antiques are expensive—for many people, prohibitively expensive. What's more, high-quality antiques are hard to come by; museums or private collectors have snapped them up, and they are unavailable at any price. But if you love the fine craftsmanship and pleasing lines of antiques, don't despair. Handsome reproductions and creative adaptations of past styles offer an excellent alternative to the scarce and costly "real thing."

You might well ask, just what *is* a reproduction? How does it differ from an antique? And what is an adaptation? In the strictest sense of the word, a reproduction is a replica of an original antique. An adaptation, however, has had modifications made—in terms of scale, function, even comfort—to meet modern-day standards and expectations.

Reproductions and adaptations are available in both machine-made and handcrafted versions. Handcrafted pieces usually cost more and look more authentic than machine-made items. In fact, you'd have a difficult time distinguishing the finest reproductions from original classic pieces, thanks to master craftsmen who hand-copy construction and decorative details.

Although good reproductions are by no means inexpensive, they generally cost less than their antique equivalents—and they're much easier to find. An ardent antique purist might disagree, but about the only discernible difference between a fine antique and a high-quality reproduction of the same piece is age. And, because today's reproductions are made to last a lifetime and longer, they may well become the antiques of tomorrow.

The widespread popularity of classically styled new furniture goes beyond cost, age, and availability considerations, however. A good reproduction or adaptation offers elegance without ostentation, formality without stiffness. Like the real thing, a new/old piece brings a sense of permanence—a comforting link to the past.

A major advantage of owning classic furnishings—be they antiques, reproductions, or sensitively modified adaptations—is their wonderful compatibility with other design styles. The timeless beauty of a single piece or a combination of a few seemingly disparate pieces may be all that's needed to impart a touch of warmth and tradition to a room setting.

The living room shown *at left* is furnished with a pleasing balance of present and past, highlighted by new versions of old classics. The pine secretary exactly replicates an old American piece, as does the corner chair, with its turned legs and rush seat. A brand-new old-fashioned wing chair (an adaptation scaled for today's standards of comfort) coexists nicely with contemporary lounge chairs and a sleek chrome-and-glass coffee table. An authentic antique rocking horse adds a touch of whimsy to the scheme.

Pick a period

Antique reproductions come in a wide variety of styles, including English, French, and American. Many eighteenth-century English and American pieces—such as the refined classics of Queen Anne, Chippendale, and Hepplewhite—are especially noted for their grace, comfort, and sturdiness.

Among the most popular of eighteenth-century designs are wing chairs, love seats, splat-back chairs, canopy beds, drop-leaf tables, highboys, lowboys, and butler's tables. All of these pieces are as practical as they are eye-pleasing, and they make sense for the way we live today.

(continued)

The nostalgically evocative oak dresser shown above is a simplified, scaled-down adaptation of an 1800s-style piece. Its small size and spare ornamentation make it appropriate for today's smaller rooms.

The comb-back writing-arm chair shown above is another example of handcrafted reproduction furniture. Like its antique ancestor, it combines distinctive character with comfort and practicality. The austere clock is true to its Shaker design roots.

The three reproduction pieces pictured here combine the casual appeal of pine with timeless, traditional design. All three—the sunburst mirror, the chest of drawers, and the Chippendale armchair—have been waxed instead of stained to bring out the beautiful grain of the wood.

FURNISHING WITH REPRODUCTIONS AND ADAPTATIONS
(continued)

Whether your taste leans toward traditional, country, or eclectic decorating, you've probably purchased—or considered—at least one piece of furniture whose ancestry goes back to another century. Whether the piece is really old or just looks that way, it owes a lot to the past. As demand for old-style furnishings increases, more and more pieces that copy or resemble yesterday's classics become available. Here are just a few that you're likely to find in stores and mail-order catalogs.

Handcrafted pieces like the handsome stepped-back china cupboard pictured above are meant to be cherished for years to come. This cupboard features a blue-painted interior perfect for showcasing favorite collections. The lower sections offer plenty of space for storing tableware and linens.

FINDING TODAY'S HANDCRAFTED FURNITURE

Besides antiques, there are other types of furniture you're unlikely to find in conventional furniture stores. Custom-made and other handcrafted furniture, made by local craftspeople and artisans, must be sought out, or just "happened upon." Custom-made furniture is specifically constructed to suit one customer's individual needs. Handcrafted items aren't necessarily made for any one particular person, but are limited in number. Look in your local Yellow Pages for listings of furniture makers and similar skilled artisans. Handcrafted items are most often found at small galleries, at crafts shows, and through mail-order catalogs.

This updated version of a traditional ladder-back chair was designed and made—by hand—out of cherry wood by a North Carolina craftswoman. The chair features hand-cut joinery and a hand-woven rush seat. Visit crafts fairs and research local woodworker-artisans if you'd like to purchase a one-of-a-kind wood piece.

Pictured below are two examples of country furniture, handcrafted in time-honored traditional style. The apothecary chest is Shaker in feeling; the gateleg drop-leaf table combines a good, old idea with contemporary sleekness. As with the chair at right, you can commission pieces from local craftspeople; crafts fairs and specialty stores are other sources.

Here are two examples of custom-styled furniture, both made of clear, ¾-inch-thick acrylic. Look in your area Yellow Pages under "plastics" or "acrylic manufacturers" to order pieces specially designed or made to your specifications.

BUYING AND CARING FOR ANTIQUES

If you've only recently started making the rounds of antique shows, estate sales, and secondhand shops, you may feel unsure about how to judge the condition and pedigree of some of the pieces you see. You may not even know the right questions to ask. Or perhaps you're an old hand at browsing but have only recently reached the point where you'd like to buy a marble-topped Victorian table or a pine blanket chest—and aren't sure why prices vary so much. Here are some basic guidelines and background information that will make you more knowledgeable about buying old furniture and antiques—and about caring for antiques after you bring them home.

As time passes, more and more furniture items become a century old and qualify, in the United States, as antiques. But just because an item is antique by definition does not necessarily mean it's valuable.

Price differences

When you shop for antiques, you may be surprised at how much prices vary from place to place and piece to piece. Some of the disparity comes from the dealers involved, but other differences reflect real factors in the furniture's quality and background.

• *Condition.* Understandably, a piece of furniture in mint condition commands a higher price than one in need of restoration or repair.

• *Material.* Antique furniture made of fine woods such as walnut, mahogany, or cherry appreciates in value faster than those of woods such as oak or pine (although the recent interest in country decorating has increased the price of these pieces, too). Accent materials, such as brass or silver hardware and leaded or beveled glass, also can raise the cost.

• *Authenticity.* When a piece is signed, dated, or in some other way documented, whether to record age, place of manufacture, or ownership, expect to pay top dollar for the pedigree. A key indicator of authenticity is shape, that is, balance and proportion. Study drawings and photographs of the "real thing" to get a sense of how an authentic piece should look.

• *Quality.* Any well-designed piece, crafted of fine materials, is a choice find, and likely to be costly. Look for the same signs of quality in antiques as you'd expect in modern pieces (see Chapter 5, "Shopping Sense").

• *Availability.* The scarcer or rarer a piece is, the more sought after and more expensive it's likely to be.

• *Source and origin.* If the piece was made by a famous craftsman, or once owned by someone of note, expect the price to be higher than usual.

Where to shop

Auctions, estate sales, and stores that specialize in antiques are the best places to look for antique furniture. You may hear of someone's finding a prize at a flea market or garage sale, but the chances of this happening are slim.

The secret to auction buying is to know what you want and what you're willing to pay, then stick to that figure. Here are some other guidelines to use at an auction or an estate sale.

• Before the sale, obtain a catalog or description of the items to be sold. In addition to information about the pieces to be auctioned, you'll find important facts such as the conditions of the sale. These explain the arrangements for payment, how soon after purchase buyers must remove pieces from the auction site, and the responsibilities of both the buyer and the auctioneer.

• Arrive at the auction early so you'll have enough time to inspect the items you're interested in. Plan to spend several hours to a whole day at an auction. Cutting yourself short on time may mean having to leave before the item you want is put up for bidding.

• Make the rounds and check out each piece of furniture at close range. If you find a piece in need of repair, figure in the repair cost before deciding what your bid will be. Never bid on an item you haven't thoroughly inspected. You may not see flaws or missing pieces from a distance.

• Be sure you understand how many items you're bidding on. Is it two chairs or just one?

• Make a note of the exact amount of your winning bid, and always keep track of your bidding number.

• Get a receipt for all payments. Generally, the auction price should be about two-thirds of what you'd pay for the piece in an antique shop.

• If you're particularly interested in acquiring a certain piece of furniture, try not to appear overly eager. Showing too much interest could tip off the auctioneer, who might manipulate the bidding to take advantage of your eagerness.

Care tips

Although antique furnishings, require no excessive care and upkeep, you should take certain steps to maintain the condition of old pieces. Most important, remember that wood is extremely sensitive to too much heat and humidity; too little moisture can be equally damaging. If your house suffers from unfavorable climatic conditions, you'd be wise to correct the problem.

Dust frequently, but be sure you're not harming the surface while removing abrasive particles. Never use cheesecloth unless you're sure all the sizing has been washed out. A polish-treated cloth is good for a polished finish, but it may soften the wax on a waxed finish. Always dust with the grain of the wood.

Polish and wax only once every few months with a liquid polish or a paste wax. Let liquid dry, then buff. Paste wax requires rubbing to bring out the sheen. If your antique piece becomes scratched or stained, check with a knowledgeable antique dealer before proceeding with a questionable first-aid remedy.

MINIATURES

IDENTIFYING ANTIQUES

Whether you want to fill your home with authentic period pieces or just want one antique for an accent, the first step toward making a good selection is to brush up on past design periods. This chart is a good place to start. It identifies five major American style periods and some design characteristics that distinguish each. The chart can help you pinpoint the style of antique that fits in best with your taste. To learn more, we suggest you read books about antiques and visit museums that have furniture collections. Talking to antique dealers in your area will tell you what's available—and what it costs—locally.

AMERICAN DESIGN PERIODS
17TH, 18TH, AND 19TH CENTURIES

EARLY AMERICAN
Early 1600s-1720

History. The early settlers' concern with the basics of life, such as shelter, food, and clothing, left little time to design elaborate furnishings. Instead, they constructed furniture that would meet their day-to-day needs and withstand hard use and frequent moving. The colonists were greatly influenced by their European ancestors. Many of the early English colonists styled their furnishings after Jacobean and William and Mary pieces from their homeland. Today, most of the remaining Early American furniture is housed in museums or private collections.

Characteristics. When compared with furnishings from later periods, Early American furniture is massive, blocky, and sturdy. The pieces are generally made of woods readily available to the settlers—pine, beech, maple, elm, ash, cherry, cedar, and cypress. Although decoration was not a prime concern, some early chests have crudely carved panels, and chairs often have turned legs and spindles like the example sketched *below.* For added strength, legs were braced with stretchers usually positioned close to the floor. Fine upholstery fabrics were scarce, so chairs typically have woven rush or wooden seats.

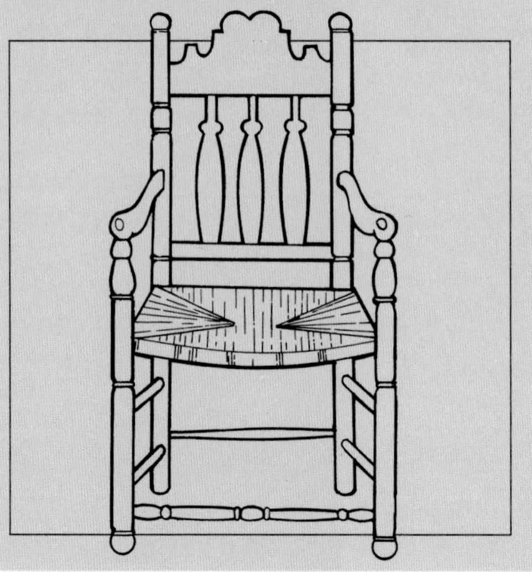

GEORGIAN
1720-1790

History. As the colonists prospered, the decoration of their homes became more important. Many Americans strove to re-create the luxury of fine English houses, and began purchasing furniture for its style as well as its use. Although American furniture makers became masters at their craft, the English still set the major trends. Important influences included Queen Anne, Georgian, and Chippendale styles. Although original Georgian pieces are priced out of reach for most people, many fine reproductions of furnishings from this period are available at prices today's average consumer can afford.

Characteristics. The furniture from this period is a great deal more refined than examples from earlier times. Graceful curves replaced straight lines, and the heavy, ponderous scale of Early American furniture gave way to a new lightness. Improved construction methods negated the need for heavy, cumbersome stretchers, so chair legs took on new, refined forms. Finely executed decoration was integrated into many furniture designs. Deep-tone hardwoods, such as walnut, mahogany, and satinwood, grew in popularity and underscored the new sense of sophistication.

FEDERAL

1790-1820

History. After the American Revolution, the new nation looked to ancient Rome and Greece for inspiration. This interest in the classics spilled over into architecture and furniture design. Symmetry, simplicity, and refinement became evident in the decors of the day, and furniture took on a delicate, streamlined look. Both George Hepplewhite and Thomas Sheraton, publishers of widely used furniture guides of the day, gave their names to this period's styles. Fine "period" pieces of the Federal style now cost thousands of dollars. Finely crafted reproductions are readily available and affordable, however.

Characteristics. The exuberant styles of the late Georgian period gave way to more delicate forms during the Federal period. Simple geometric shapes were used for chair backs. Legs were typically slender and tapered; although some carving was still done, detailed veneers and inlays decorated the surfaces of many tables and chests instead. In keeping with the preference for a lighter scale, light-color satinwood gained popularity over mahogany and walnut.

EMPIRE

1820-1860

History. As the country grew and people became more affluent, architecture and furniture were once again designed on a large, grand scale. Americans adapted the styles of the French Napoleonic empire, too. One of the era's best-known furniture makers was Duncan Phyfe, who produced restrained but elegant Empire designs. Mechanized factories began replacing the craftsmen's workshops, making fashionable furniture available at every price level.

Characteristics. American Empire furnishings are typically more simple and less ornate than the French pieces they were adapted from. Many Roman and Egyptian motifs popular in France, for instance, were omitted in the United States. And instead of heavy bronze mountings, brass ornamentation embellished American furniture. Motifs commonly used included concave-curved legs ending in animal feet like those shown *below*, squat-lyre forms, scrolled legs, and reeded columns. Late Empire designs became bulky and ponderous, as Americans turned toward the next new style, Victorian.

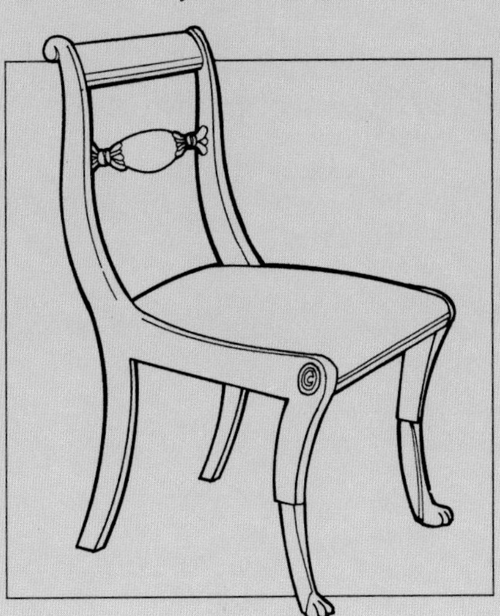

VICTORIAN

1840-1890

History. Industry and new technology flourished, but interest in the arts waned during this period. A slump in taste standards encouraged a spate of mass-produced furnishings, many poorly constructed and gaudy in design. Eclecticism dominated architectural and decorative works; influences came from Gothic, French Rococo, and Romanesque styles. Good antique Victorian pieces are popular today, but are still affordable.

Characteristics. As homes became larger and more luxurious, furniture, too, became bigger and more elaborately decorated. Although carvings and turnings were lavishly used in this period, they were done with less finesse than in the past. Intricate Gothic tracery and deeply carved rococo scrolls, garlands, and shells decorated chair backs, legs, and table skirts. Chairs with high balloon backs, like the one shown *below*, upholstered in rich velvets and leathers, were popular for parlors. Dark woods, such as mahogany and walnut, were favored early in the Victorian period; later, oak and other light woods became the norm.

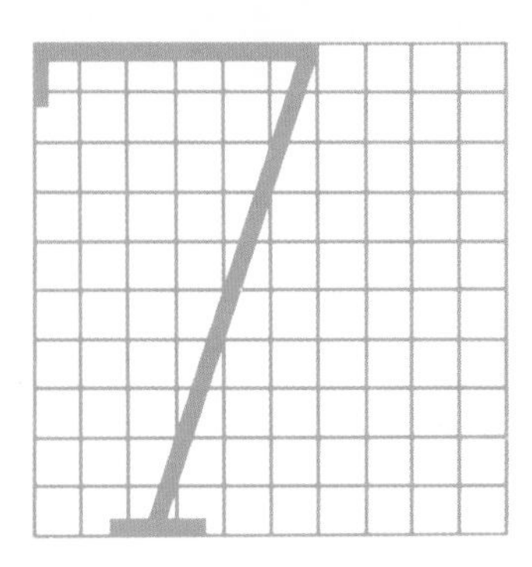

OUTDOOR FURNITURE

Whether you use outdoor furniture outside on a deck, porch, or patio, or inside in a family room or solarium, its easygoing style invites relaxation. And the durable, no-fuss materials that help it withstand the elements make it a breeze to live with, indoors as well as out. In this chapter, we'll show you some of the styles and materials that are common to outdoor furniture. Along the way, we'll give you shopping and maintenance pointers, and some ideas for using this kind of furniture in your yard, on your porch, or inside your home.

ALL-WEATHER FURNITURE

Take a look at the two photos shown here, and you'll see how the right furnishings can make any yard or patio a summer-long vacation spot. These examples also illustrate two of the several types of outdoor furnishings you'll want to become familiar with before you go shopping.

The shady outdoor living room, or lanai, pictured *opposite* is an ideal spot for breakfast or snacks. The modestly priced stacking chairs are made of tubular aluminum with vinyl strapping. The chairs are not only lightweight, but also maintenance free, with materials meant to take a lot of sun, rain, and heavy use. For relief from the sun's rays, consider making a do-it-yourself canopy. Here, ready-made snow fencing was tacked to a wooden frame.

In the yard, two matching chaise longues provide sunbathing comfort, and a handy hammock hangs between two obliging trees.

The brick patio, *below,* gains its high-style comfort from woven metal-mesh furnishings. The chairs and a table with a tempered-glass top have an airy look that makes them perfect for even a small deck or patio.

For sink-in comfort, these chairs have specially designed cushions that let the rain run right through them.

(continued)

ALL-WEATHER FURNITURE

(continued)

Outdoor furniture can be as rustic as the home-built redwood picnic set shown *opposite* or as high-tech-slick as the steel-framed, epoxy-coated table and chairs pictured *at right.* Whether you shop for simple wood pieces or designer-elegant ensembles, you'll find furnishings that can hold their own against the elements in a wide range of materials, styles, and prices. Here's a brief rundown of the most popular options.

- *Aluminum* furniture is lightweight, sturdy, and economical. It usually has simple, clean lines and colorful webbing or vinyl-coated fabric cushions. Although tubular aluminum is the most common, you'll also find solid-bar aluminum and cast aluminum pieces; all three types are virtually maintenance free.
- Generally more expensive than aluminum, *wrought-iron* furnishings often feature ornate curlicues and other fanciful designs. Their airy, delicate looks, however, belie a durable, heavy structure.
- *Steel* furnishings sometimes have a nostalgic look, too, although they tend to have less ornamentation than their wrought-iron counterparts. Steel pieces also come in a range of contemporary styles.
- Another all-weather option is *wood* furniture, which comes in a wide variety of prices. The top of the line is *redwood,* which resists warping and splitting. The least expensive wood pieces are made of pine or other white woods, such as cedar or cottonwood; these can be good buys, but won't last as long as redwood.

Whatever all-weather furniture you select, bear in mind that it will last longer if you store it inside during winter.

OUTDOOR FURNITURE

PORCH FURNITURE

The breezy tropical look of basket furniture and the casual appeal of simple wooden pieces can turn any porch into an inviting retreat. Whether used on a screened porch or a covered patio, these furnishings enjoy the outdoors, but they need some protection from sun and rain.

With their lighthearted, natural appeal, *wicker furnishings* have long been porch favorites. They mix easily with other furnishing styles and materials, and require little maintenance. Designs range from straightforward pieces, such as those shown *at left*, to intricate, airy weaves with a romantic Victorian flavor.

The term "wicker" refers to furnishings made by weaving strips of a tropical plant (such as rattan, raffia, buri, reed, or willow) around a rattan frame. Often pieces are lacquered or painted to help seal the natural fiber strips against dust and dirt.

Like other furniture woven of organic materials—sometimes called "basket furniture"—wicker needs shielding from too much direct sunlight. (Sunshine dries out the fiber, hastening deterioration.) The delightful deck shown *at left*, for example, sports a movable canvas sun screen that shelters a pair of natural wicker armchairs and a matching glass-topped table. The covering slides back to let in the sun, yet when drawn it shades the deck and protects the furnishings.

Wicker also needs protection from soaking rain. (Here the canvas covering shields the pieces during a light rain, but the furnishings are carried inside during heavy storms.)

When you shop for wicker pieces, you may find imitation wicker made from twisted paper or plastic. If a man-made version of wicker has been lacquered, it's often hard to distinguish from the real thing. For specific buymanship information about wicker, see pages 111-113.

(continued)

PORCH FURNITURE
(continued)

In addition to wicker, other kinds of basket furniture are well suited to porch life.

• *Rattan* furnishings, made from the solid vine or stem of a climbing jungle palm, are solid and strong. Rattan is sturdy enough to be nailed at joints, yet flexible enough to be steamed and bent into delightfully curving shapes. Scorched rattan has a multitone finish that resembles tortoiseshell and is made by browning the rattan with a torch.

• *Cane,* the outer skin of rattan split into strands, usually is woven—while wet—into the seats and backs of seating pieces.

• *Bamboo* is often mistaken for rattan. Unlike solid rattan, however, bamboo is hollow and therefore weaker and less flexible. Bamboo furniture can be attractive, but it needs careful handling for maximum wear.

Good companions for basket furniture—and solid choices for porch furnishings—are *hardwood* pieces. Probably the most popular example is the classic director's chair.

Two ways to treat a porch

The two porches shown here are good examples of sheltered areas where these furnishings can function safely, year after year. *Opposite,* budget-price wicker seating pieces and a natural fiber rug from an import store create a stylish retreat.

The screened porch pictured *at right* includes a mix of wicker and painted wooden pieces. An antique wicker settee, a green pub table, and matching Windsor chairs comfortably share space with contemporary director's chairs. Plastic window blinds help fend off rain, and let the owners use furnishings here that would otherwise deteriorate in inclement weather.

USING OUTDOOR FURNITURE INDOORS

Although many of today's outdoor furnishings are destined for porch, patio, or poolside, they're equally at home inside. The comfortable feel and look of seating and storage pieces in this category make them welcome almost anywhere. Here are some ideas for making the most of your outdoor furnishings all year long, inside as well as out.

When it comes to using outdoor furniture indoors, few rules apply. Wicker, aluminum, wrought iron, mesh, canvas, redwood, and other outdoor-oriented materials can easily harmonize with many other strictly indoor pieces. Together they'll create a vibrant mix of textures and colors.

You're used to planning groupings of conventional indoor furniture for compatibility of style, color, and scale. And you'll want to select your outdoor furniture the same way. Choose pieces that blend easily into your rooms and that fit in with other furnishings.

You may find it easiest to create a cohesive grouping of inviting, warm-weather favorites in a family room or den, for example. Then add baskets, plants, and other natural touches for a year-long feeling of summertime.

Eclectic bedfellows

You also can try using just one or more porch or patio pieces as distinctive accents. The old-house bedroom pictured *at right* is a good example of a successful indoor-outdoor mix.

Graceful wicker furniture pieces like these used to line Victorian verandas, and they're still popular. You can easily find them in many furniture stores and catalogs. When airy, handwoven chairs, settees, and tables come indoors, they add gracious comfort and old-fashioned charm.

In this eclectic setting, the painted wicker works with the white curtains and pillowcases to provide crisp contrast to the dark wood floor, chest, and four-poster bed. The bright-red cushions tie the wicker pieces in with the old quilts and the area rug. *(continued)*

USING OUTDOOR FURNITURE INDOORS

(continued)

A glance at the three photos here should convince you about the versatility of today's "outdoor" furniture. It's easy to envision these pieces in their customary patio or poolside settings, but they also work beautifully indoors in a living room, family room, or bay window.

The handsome teak park bench shown *opposite* has no trouble moving inside. Its classic styling, attractive grain, and high-quality construction make it a natural when you need extra seating in an informal entry hall, a family room, or a plant-filled bay like the one shown here.

The second example, *at right,* makes it clear that fireside comfort needn't be limited to an overstuffed easy chair or a conventionally upholstered lounge chair and ottoman. A beautifully designed chaise longue like this invites feet-up fireside relaxing. And when warm weather arrives, this lightweight piece moves outdoors easily.

The reclining chaise has an open-weave seat and back, and it self-adjusts for optimum comfort. Best of all, its elegant lines and sculptured-looking frame make it perfect for crisp, contemporary settings such as this one.

Other outdoor furnishings offer the sink-in comfort of plump cushions. In addition to thick seat and back cushions, the lounge chair pictured *at left* also features a network of webs underneath each cushion to provide flexible support. Upholstered in an easy-care grid-pattern fabric, the clean-lined chair (it comes with a matching ottoman, not shown) makes an attractive addition to this contemporary family room.

BUYING AND CARING FOR OUTDOOR FURNITURE

Your choice of outdoor furniture—whether it be elaborate wrought iron, sleek aluminum, or rustic wicker—should be more than just a matter of taste. Where and how you plan to use the furnishings also should influence your decision. How exposed will they be to the weather? Do you expect to be moving the pieces frequently? What does it take to keep the material in top condition? On these pages we'll give you pointers about recognizing sound construction and choosing appropriate furnishings for the settings you plan. Outdoor furniture by definition needs a minimum of care. All the same, it benefits from a few simple maintenance steps, which you'll find in the chart that follows on pages 112 and 113.

Because there's such a variety of versatile outdoor furniture, it's important to decide how and where you intend to use the pieces before you make your selections. For instance, if you plan to use a chaise longue outdoors in summer, moving it frequently from one place to another, a lightweight piece (such as one made from tubular aluminum) may be your best bet.

Or, if you're in the market for a grouping of casual furniture primarily for your family room, but you also intend to occasionally use the pieces on an open sundeck, you'll want to buy pieces that are sun- and rain-resistant.

Whatever your needs, don't stint on quality. Cheap outdoor furniture can turn into junk in just a couple of seasons. Here's what to look for—and look out for—when selecting outdoor pieces.

Rattan, bamboo, wicker, and cane

If you buy wisely, with high-quality construction and classic design in mind, you can count on years of enjoyment from basket pieces.

One of the first things to look for when buying rattan is discoloration or physical defects. Do the pieces look solid and sturdy? Next, check the finish—is it smooth, hard, and free of fuzz?

Although nodes (growth marks) are part of the charm of rattan and bamboo pieces, look for pieces with nodes that are 12 to 18 inches apart and uniform in size. These pieces will have a smoother, less "knobby" look than lower-quality pieces, and they probably will be sturdier, too.

Check the joints to be sure they're close-fitting and secured firmly with glue, nails, or screws. Also, see whether the joints have bindings of genuine peel (the tough outer bark of the rattan pole) for additional strength. Plastic bindings indicate inexpensive pieces—and inferior quality.

When selecting a table, look for tabletop moldings set flush with the top, and mitered corners; these features show superior construction. The whole piece should be balanced, stable, and free of wobbles.

Finally, check the strap supports under any cushions; they should attach securely to a separate seat frame, not directly to the rattan or bamboo.

Aluminum

Because today's aluminum is virtually maintenance free and economical, it's one of the most popular outdoor-furniture materials.

Most new aluminum furniture is rustproof, but to be on the safe side, make sure any unpainted aluminum piece you buy has been anodized to protect it from rusting.

Many pieces are constructed with tubular frames. The thicker the walls of the tubes, the stronger the frame. Thick, heavy pieces will hold up best in hard-use areas. However, if you plan to move a piece frequently, you may prefer a lighter one; just make sure it's balanced and stable so it won't tip over.

(continued)

BUYING AND CARING FOR OUTDOOR FURNITURE

(continued)

When shopping for outdoor furniture, you're also likely to come across expensive, heavy furniture made of solid aluminum bars or cast aluminum.

Some aluminum pieces are flexible and fold for storage; others have welded joints. Frame edges and welds should be smooth, and welded joints should be strong. If the furniture folds, be sure the hinges have been plated to retard rust. Try out folding chairs and tables to make sure they hold their positions safely.

Finally, look for rubber or plastic tips or glides on legs to protect indoor flooring, and make sure any attached fabrics are inserted securely into welded frames.

Wrought iron and steel

Be especially careful when buying these pieces; some collections of wrought iron and steel are intended only for indoor use. If you plan to use the furniture outdoors, ask whether it has been treated with a rust inhibitor and given a primer coat. Check the finish; it should be smooth, without a bubbly appearance.

All wrought iron is welded, and so is much steel furniture. Examine the welds to make sure that they're smooth and that they securely encircle each joint. Instead of welds, some quick-assembly steel pieces are held together with rivets, screws, or bolts. Make sure these fasteners don't have rough edges, and are positioned so they won't snag clothing.

As with aluminum furnishings, look for rubber or plastic tips or glides on the legs to protect your flooring.

Redwood

The highest-quality redwood furniture is made from the heart of the wood, then treated with a stain and sealer to produce furniture with uniform texture and color. High-quality pieces also are especially strong, because they are made with knot-free wood. As with conventional furniture, the best construction features mortise-and-tenon joints reinforced with glue. In less-costly pieces, you may find that joints have been merely nailed and that no sealer was applied over the stain.

When looking at redwood pieces, check that edges have been sanded smooth and that corners have been rounded to protect clothing. Also, is any visible hardware rust resistant? If the furnishings have any knots, be sure they are sound and tight.

Much redwood furniture is shipped only partially assembled. Look for pieces that have easy-to-follow assembly instructions.

Hardwood

If your choice is a classic director's chair, sit on it to make sure it's sturdy, level, and rigid enough to provide good support.

Besides chairs, you'll find a range of tables, accessories, and stools in this category. You'll also find hardwoods used on some metal outdoor furniture, often to form arms. Finishes include stains, paints, and natural varnishes.

When you buy hardwood furniture, check to see that frames are smooth and uniform, and are sanded to a fine silky finish. For more about selecting hardwood furniture, see pages 70 and 71.

MAINTAINING OUTDOOR FURNITURE

	USES
BASKET	Basket furniture is ideal for enclosed or semi-enclosed porches. It needs some protection from rain and sun.
ALUMINUM	Aluminum is sun- and rain-resistant. Often, aluminum pieces have sleek styling for indoor and outdoor contemporary flair. If storage space is a problem, look for folding aluminum pieces.
WROUGHT IRON AND STEEL	Most wrought-iron and steel pieces work well indoors or out They are sun resistant and newer pieces usually are rust resistant, too.
REDWOOD	Because it can withstand sun and moisture, redwood is ideal for outdoor use. But its attractive appearance and sturdiness also make it suitable for your family room.
HARDWOOD	Hardwood furnishings are easily used in a family room or enclosed porch. With certain exceptions, such as teak, they should not be exposed to the elements.

GENERAL CARE	REPAIR
Don't hose off basket furniture; simply wipe with a damp cloth to clean and moisten fibers. Vacuum with a soft brush attachment to remove dust. Protect with liquid furniture wax.	Small breaks in wicker can be repaired by applying water-proof glue to the area around the break; cover with waxed paper, and clamp for 24 hours. Structural damage requires professional help.
Apply auto paste wax to frames after washing with mild detergent. Also, wax any hardwood arms. Rub unpainted aluminum frames with steel wool dipped in kerosene to brighten them.	To repair nicks and scratches on painted frames, use matching touch-up paint.
After washing with a hose to remove dust and soil, rub scratches with steel wool and apply metal primer to spot. Apply auto paste wax every year, especially to crevices and weld joints.	To remove rust, rub with a stiff wire brush, then sand with steel wool. To repaint, use good exterior enamel; its glossy finish will help shed dirt and moisture. Use epoxy cement to repair broken joints.
As with other outdoor furnishings, it's best to bring redwood indoors in winter. Also, apply one or two coats of preservative or redwood stain every year for added protection. Remove spills promptly.	If the finish wears, re-apply redwood stain and a sealer. To remove stain, such as spilled soft drinks, use household bleach or oxalic acid, then rinse thoroughly. Tighten or replace bolts and screws as needed.
To clean, wipe wood occasionally with a damp cloth. Wax wood for extra protection.	Tighten or replace screws and bolts that are loose or broken. Repaint, stain, or seal wood as needed.

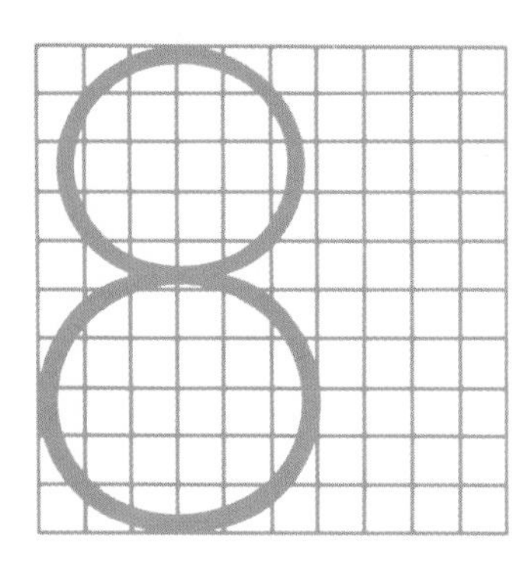

FURNITURE YOU CAN MAKE YOURSELF

Experience helps, but you really don't need woodworking skills, a basement full of tools, or upholstery know-how to craft one-of-a-kind furnishings. The secret: Plan projects you can make with a few hand tools, or a needle and thread. This chapter offers 14 examples of items that start with a few sheets of plywood, plumbing fittings, salvage store finds, unfinished furniture—even chicken coops and dish towels. At the end of the chapter you'll find a listing of the tools and hardware required for these projects. Just about everything could fit into a small toolbox.

A ROOMFUL OF EASY PIECES

Every picture tells a story, and the photo *at right* has one clear theme: easy-to-build furniture made from easy-to-get materials.

Consider the dining table, for instance. Constructed from birch plywood, it's a solid addition to almost any dwelling. Each leg is actually a plywood sandwich—two layers glued together, the joints carefully hidden by wood veneer tape. Taped-over 1x2s beneath plywood make the top look equally thick. Two angle irons secure each leg to the top. (See illustration *at bottom left* on page 117.)

To build a similar table, you'll need two sheets of ¾-inch birch plywood. Pay the lumberyard a little extra to cut the top and a single leg from one of the sheets. With a saw, cut three more legs on your own, using the original leg as a pattern. Then sandwich the pairs of legs together with white glue.

Next, drill holes every 5 or 6 inches along the length of each angle iron. To position the supports easily, draw a line ¾ inch from the top of each leg (both sides), match the top of the angle iron to this line, and attach it to the leg using flat-head wood screws.

Invert the tabletop, measure in 18 to 24 inches from each end, and draw two lines across the width of the plywood, leaving a 1½- to 2-inch space between the lines. On each side of this gap, nail on a 1x4. Later, you'll fit the legs into these slots and screw the angle irons to the 1x4s.

Keeping the table upside down, frame the top's under edge with 1x2s. Then sand any rough spots, and apply the wood veneer tape according to directions on the package.

(continued)

FUMAR EL PAPEL
JOB
Ó DEJAR DE FUMAR

A ROOMFUL OF EASY PIECES

(continued)

The versatile sofa shown *at left* is a real prize, especially for homes and apartments where space is at a premium. It's a seating piece, a sleeping piece, and—thanks to the attached end table—a serving piece, all in one. Not only that, but beneath the cushions are two roomy storage holds.

To build a sofa like this one, start with two and a half sheets of inexpensive 4x8 plywood, 25 feet of 1x2s, 1¼-inch wood screws, 1½-inch finishing nails, and enough carpet to wrap around the wood. From the plywood, build two boxes—a square one for the end table and a long, rectangular platform for the sofa. Butt-join all edges, gluing and nailing them in place. When the boxes are finished, bolt them together.

Then divide the larger box into two compartments of the same size, nail a partition between them, and cut two trap doors to fit over each opening.

Using a utility knife, cut the carpet, then glue and staple it to the boxes. Add cushions. (For more about making your own cushions, see page 120.)

More than meets the eye

Like its multitalented roommate, the coffee table pictured *opposite* is perfect for tight situations. Its attractive exterior offers plenty of surface area to handle cups, saucers, plates, and more. Inside, it can accommodate objects as large as the folding chairs shown. Casters make it a movable treat.

This table is 38 inches long, 26 inches wide, and 12½ inches high, but you can make a similar table larger or smaller to fit the furniture it goes with and your own room. Whatever the size, it's not hard to build.

Start with ¾-inch birch plywood. Cut pieces to your dimensions, or have the lumberyard do it. You'll need six pieces in all—top, two sides, back, hinged door, and storage shelf (or box bottom). Next, assemble four pieces into a partial box, leaving one end and the bottom open. Miter-join all edges.

Set the floor of the storage compartment at least ¾ inch in from the front opening. Make sure it's raised approximately an inch above the floor. If you plan to store heavy objects, you may want to use thicker, stronger plywood for the storage shelf than for the rest of the unit.

Now it's time to attach the movable front "door" of the box. We used invisible hinges but you can use a piano hinge instead. Install a catch to hold the lid shut; then attach four recessed casters.

Screw on the swinging door, and add a wooden pull. Finish to taste; a coat of polyurethane will protect your table.

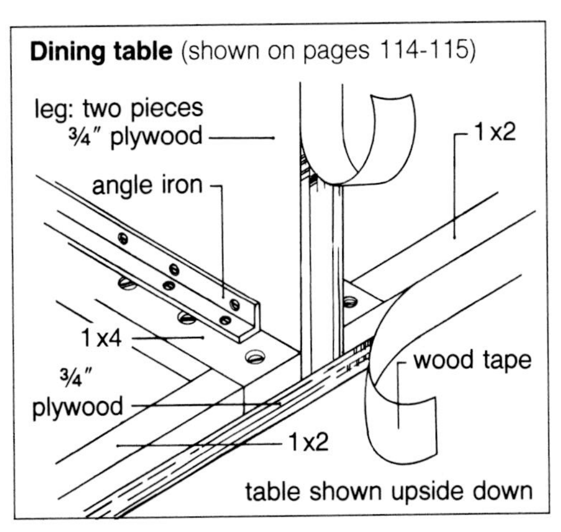

Dining table (shown on pages 114-115)

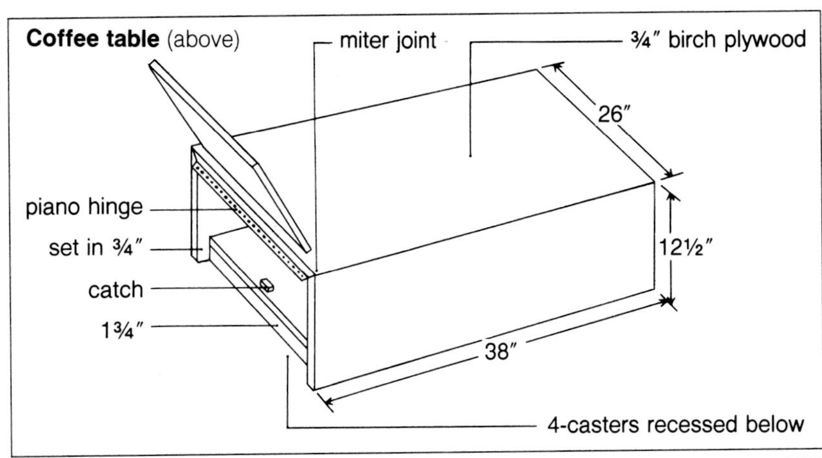

Coffee table (above)

TABLES

See-through tabletops combined with unusual bases are decorative, functional, and anything but run-of-the-mill. They're also not difficult to create. And "create" is the word for the three shown here.

The intriguingly geometric table shown *at right* illustrates one angle of this approach. The splayed-leg base is nothing more than four hefty Italian-style banisters purchased at an "architecture recycling" shop. (More about sources below.) The legs are glued in place on a ¾-inch plywood square trimmed with quarter-round molding. For further reinforcement, turn the base upside-down and screw or nail the base to the legs. Next, sand and paint, if necessary, and you're ready to add the top. This one is ¾-inch-thick glass.

The flower-crowned mahogany pedestal table in the background is topped by a ⅜-inch-thick glass circle. The base was originally a newel post from a staircase landing in a late-nineteenth-century house. To use something like this as a table base, saw the ends to make them flat, then nail on an X-shape brace made of 1x2s to support the glass. Add another X, this one made of 2x4s, to the bottom for greater stability. Refinish.

Making old things new

If you like the idea of using old building parts for homecrafted furniture, you have some legwork to do, but your search is likely to pay off eventually. Check antique stores, wrecking companies, salvage dealers, and your local newspaper's classified advertising section. You may discover enterprising entrepreneurs who specialize in selling architectural memorabilia.

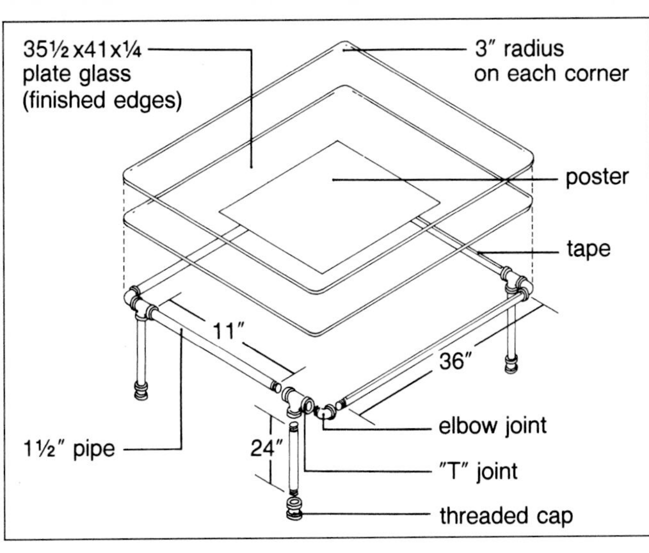

Recycled architectural items are one source for offbeat, good-looking, and functional table bases. Purchased items originally destined for technical uses are another possibility. The sleek table shown *above* rests on PVC (polyvinyl chloride) pipe—the kind plumbers use. The top is nonbreakable acrylic plastic, rounded at the edges—good features if you have young children.

To build a table like this, get some lengths of PVC pipe and cut them to size with a fine-tooth saw. Assemble all the pieces by cleaning the ends with acetone and joining them together with pipe cement. Let the connections take hold for several minutes, and then use spray enamel to paint the table any color you choose. When the paint's dry, add strips of tape along the top edge (art drafting tape or auto pinstriping tape works well).

Top the table with a layer of acrylic plastic. To emulate the design pictured here, add a poster or other piece of artwork. Simply position it on the surface, and put down another layer of acrylic plastic.

The drawing *at left* shows sizes and parts used to make this table.

CHAIRS

The cushion-covered chicken coops pictured *above* needed only a little work to turn them from what they were to what they are. Once you have similar coops (check with farm-supply outlets), just glue and nail ¾-inch cut-to-fit plywood sheets over the framing to make a base for the cushions.

The cushions shown here were made with foam slabs that are cut to fit the top of the coops. You can buy foam in various thicknesses through mail order catalogs or in fabric stores. Once you determine what size cushions you need, simply pencil the desired shape on top of the foam. Then, using an electric carving knife, carefully cut along the lines. If you want a very soft cushion, try stacking two or more thicknesses of thinner foam together.

The cushion's fabric coverings are simple to make; one long panel wraps around the cushion and is joined by two small side panels to make a box shape. The ends of the long panel simply overlap on the bottom of the cushion, making a hidden slit that allows the covering to easily slip over the foam slab.

To make each slipcover, first determine the length of fabric needed for the long panel. Do this by adding together the width and height of the foam slab, doubling this measurement, then adding 4¼ inches to allow for overlap and ease. To get the panel's width, simply measure the length of the foam slab and add 1¼ inches for ½-inch seam allowances and ease.

To determine the measurements for the two rectangular side panels, add 1 inch (for ½-inch seam allowances) to both the width and height of the slab.

With right sides joined, pin the long panel to one side panel. Overlap the ends of long panel to create the slit. Stitch the panels together, easing the corners. Then repeat with the second side panel. Turn the cover and slip it over the foam slab. Make sure the seams are straight and the corners are square.

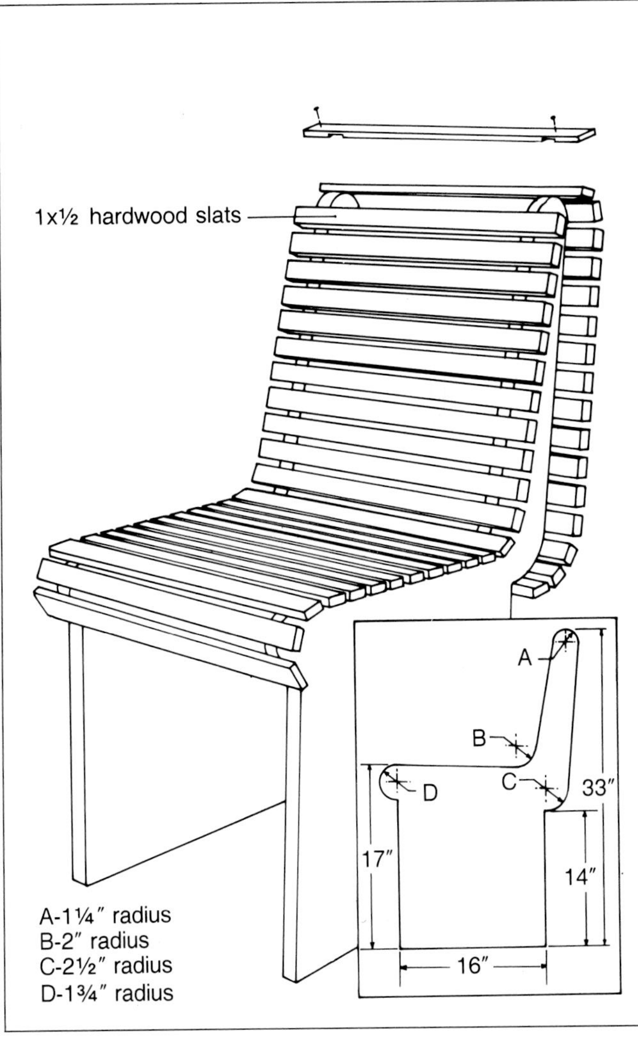

The stylish chair pictured *above* offers crisp, up-to-date design as well as body-molding comfort. And building one, or more, won't even come close to breaking your budget.

Putting the chair together requires some patience, but once you have the hang of it, making similar pieces should be a snap. This chair is 33 inches high and 18 inches wide, but you can vary the dimensions.

Start by enlarging the side pattern shown *above, right,* transferring it to a sheet of ¾-inch birch plywood. Then carefully cut out two identical shapes.

To make the slats, you'll need 1x½-inch hardwood. For this size chair, cut forty-two 18-inch lengths.

Preparing the slats so they'll fit over the side pieces is the part of the project that takes a bit of time and perseverance, especially if you're working with hand tools. Mark each slat (near both ends) for a ¾-inch-wide, 3/16-inch-deep dado, placed so it will overlap each side by 1¾ inches. Then, cut the dadoes.

If you use a router, bench saw, or radial arm saw, you can do the job much more quickly. All of these power tools make cutting dadoes a simple chore—and a much more accurate one than you could probably do by hand.

When you've finished cutting, attach the slats to the side pieces. Beginning at the lower rear, glue and nail each slat in place. Keep them parallel and the spacing consistent.

To complete the chair, sand the edges and surfaces. Then finish the wood.

EMBELLISH A BOX

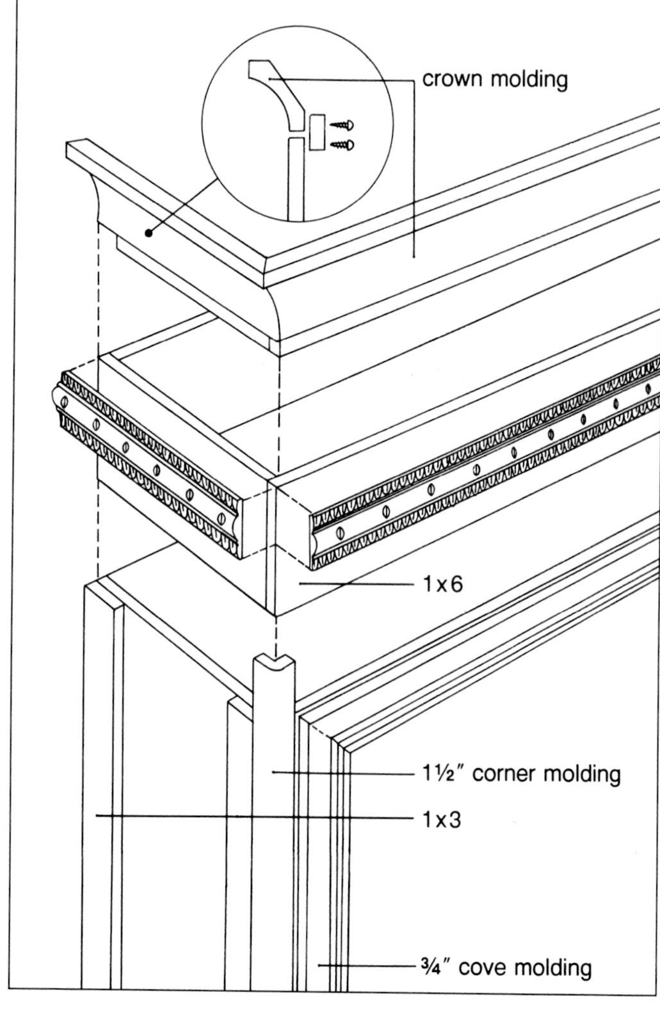

The elegant armoire shown on these two pages is little more than a ready-made box with a custom-made crown. The ornamentation, which you can easily add on your own, is the *real* cabinetmaker, transforming an unpretentious wardrobe into a presence.

To create a similar beauty, start with a visit to a store that sells unfinished furniture. Buy a standard floor cabinet with doors. The first step on the way to making it special is to nail a 1x3 vertical to each side. Next, nail 1½-inch corner molding along the right and left front edges, running it 3 inches above the top of the cabinet so the molding will cover the corners of the crown.

If you can, take the doors off their hinges, and work on them on the floor. Frame each door with a decorative molding; use 1-inch finishing nails and make sure to miter the corners. Fill nail holes and joints with matching wood putty, and sand them smooth.

Apply ⅝-inch-wide cabinet overlay molding to the doors. Along with more basic kinds of molding, you can purchase ready-made reversible arcs, straight pieces, and a variety of embossed wood carvings at most lumberyards and building supply centers.

Cut straight pieces with a coping saw, position the arcs, and nail the molding to the door, using putty as before. Then nail on the embossed woodwork wherever you want.

To top off the project, make the crown. Use 1x6s to fashion a simple box, and decorate as you like. For this armoire, cove molding (on top), block pattern molding, and two strips of scrollwork molding fill the bill.

The next-to-finishing touch is to place the crown atop the cabinet. Here an embossed wood carving, centered over the doors, and two flanking embossed fans are the icing on a richly decorated cake.

With a piece as fanciful as this, you have a free hand when it comes to finishing the wood. Stain it, seal it and leave it natural as shown *above* and *opposite,* even antique it. You'll find a wide color range to choose from.

EMBELLISH A BOX
(continued)

If you need work space that looks—and is—efficient, try this: Take a plain, ordinary file cabinet, and turn it into a movable mini-desk, like the one shown *opposite.*

Start with a well-built wood or metal cabinet; you may be able to get one secondhand from an office supply store at a good price.

To build the flip top, begin by cutting three rectangles from ½-inch plywood. The middle piece should be wide enough to both cover the top of the cabinet and hide the support brackets.

Cut the two side pieces so they're about 15 inches long and equal in width to the middle section. Using piano hinges, attach them to the middle piece.

Place the desk top on the cabinet, and anchor it in position with wood screws or metal bolts. Then bolt or screw two drop-leaf table supports beneath each side piece.

To finish the project, use screws or bolts to add furniture casters at each corner of the cabinet's base. Paint or stain, according to taste.

Here's another way to turn a basic metal cabinet into a brilliant new addition to your home. Behind closed doors, the handsome dresser shown *above* is nothing more than two sets of utility shelves, the kind meant for organizing things in a basement or garage.

To make the doors, hinge two panels of a lattice screen together, and attach them to each side. (Piano hinges will do fine in both cases.) If necessary, cut the legs off the screen beforehand, and make sure to adjust the bottom shelf so it fits flush with the bottom of the screen.

Hiding the sides is no problem. Using stove bolts and finish washers, attach ¼-inch tempered hardboard panels to the metal frame.

If the screen's a little too narrow, screw one or more 1x2s at the point where the doors meet, as shown in the illustration *at right.* Adding magnetic catches will help keep the screens in place. As a final touch, attach wooden pulls to the doors.

One pleasant note: When it's time to move on, the dresser disassembles as easily as it goes together.

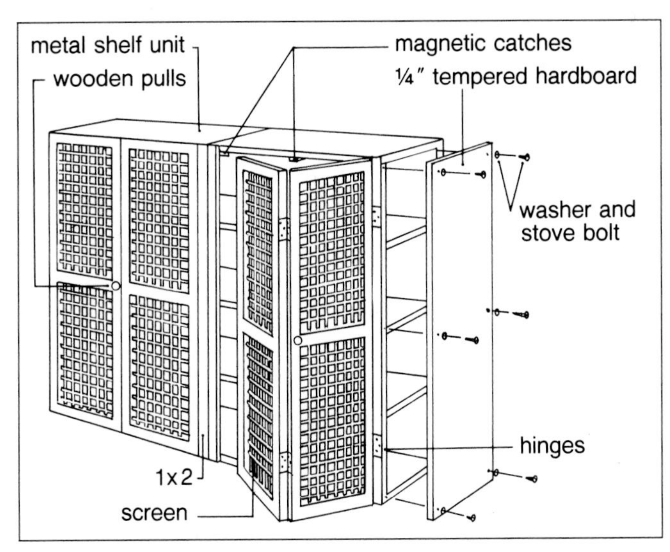

FURNITURE YOU CAN MAKE YOURSELF

BEDS AND COVERS

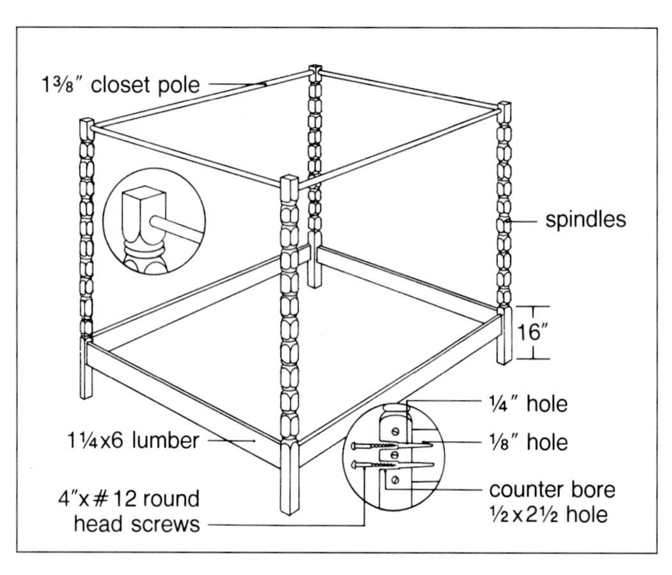

The traditional charm of this bedroom helps to make a relaxingly dreamy rest stop. One big reason for the airy, open look is the magnificent four-poster bed. Too expensive? Not at all. And, you can build one just like it in an afternoon, in time to settle down for a good night's sleep.

You won't, of course, *make* the spindles—you can find them at nearly any lumberyard. Once you have them, you're ready to begin. Using 1¼x6-inch lumber, cut end- and sideboards equal in size to the box spring.

Anchor the spindles to the boards. Counterbore two ½x2½-inch holes into the edges of the lumber and the connecting faces at the base of each spindle, as shown in the illustration *above*. Secure the spindles to the boards with 4-inch-long No. 12 round-head screws.

Then, as illustrated in the drawing, join the tops of the spindles, using 1⅜-inch closet poles. To finish your bed, stain or paint the wood.

Part of what makes this bed so alluring is the linen quilt almost floating atop it. To make a similar covering for a double bed, you'll need 12 dish towels (24x33 inches each), a backing sheet (or 12 more towels for a reversible quilt), sheet-size polyester-fiberfill quilt batting (nine thicknesses went into this one), and colored yarn for tufting.

Sew the dish towels into a giant patchwork; then seam the patchwork to the backing around three sides, right sides together. The backing, of course, must be made the same size.

Arrange layers of fiberfill batting on top of the wrong-side-out cover. Then loosely hand-stitch the batting to the three seam allowances and along the top edge of the open side, making sure not to sew towels and sheet together. Turn right side out, and hand-sew the opening closed.

To make the tufts, cut 8-inch lengths of yarn, and sew—using a wide-eyed needle—from the top through the batting and backing, and then back up and out. Knot and tie bows.

GLASS CLOTH

BEDS AND COVERS
(continued)

A simple bed like the one shown *at left* is an inexpensive but striking alternative to more conventional sleeping quarters. Just take a conventional spring and a metal frame, and build a box around them, using three hollow-core doors and, at the headboard end, a less costly 1x4 crosspiece that doesn't show. Add a mattress, and you have a dramatic sleep space.

To build a bed like this one, start with three 15-inch hollow-core doors, cut to fit around the box spring. Plug the cut-off ends of each door with a block of wood glued in place.

Then join the doors by countersinking 3-inch wood screws, as shown in the illustration *at right.* When you've completed three sides of the box, fill over the screw heads with wood putty.

Cut a 1x4 crosspiece to fit on the headboard side, and attach it with metal corner brackets.

Paint with a semigloss enamel, let dry, and simply place your mattress and box spring inside the box.

You can, of course, add a headboard, if you wish. Here, it's not really a board at all, but a dramatic-looking paint job that creates the same effect—at a much lower price.

To top everything off, the bedspread is also a bargain when compared to ready-made quilted cover-ups. Make it from the kind of prequilted fabric used in ski jackets, joining the lengths together at the quilting lines to hide the seams from view.

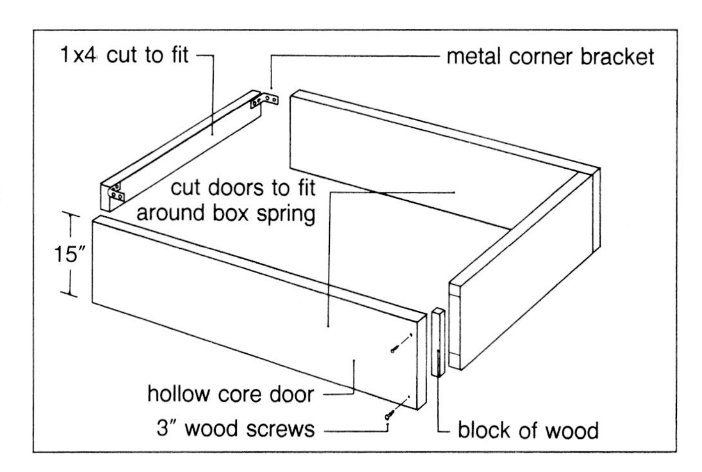

A FURNITURE BUILDER'S TOOLBOX

All the projects described in this chapter are easy to build using a basic array of tools and hardware:

- *Hammer.* A 13-ounce curved-claw hammer is best for most jobs.
- *Screwdrivers.* Three or four screwdrivers of varying sizes—including one small Phillips—should be enough.
- *Adjustable wrenches.* Keep both a 6- and a 9-inch wrench handy.
- *Push drill.* This is used to start holes for screws, and often is easier to work with than an electric drill.
- *Combination square.* You'll need this to position right angles. Also use it to measure 45-degree angles for miter joints.
- *Block plane.* Use it on rough wood edges or pieces that don't quite fit.
- *Staple gun.* This is a must if you're attaching fabric to a wood frame. Use ¼- or ½-inch staples.
- *Power drill.* A ⅜-inch model is the best choice, although ¼- and ½-inch drills also will do the job. Make sure your drill works in reverse and operates at variable speeds. With the proper bits, it becomes a power screwdriver.
- *Portable electric saber saw.* Generally, finer blades yield smoother edges.
- *Nails.* Nails come in a broad variety of sizes and shapes. For most of the projects in this chapter, you'll use slender finishing or casing nails. To attach molding to furniture, smaller brad nails are best.
- *Screws.* When fastening wood to wood or wood to metal, use flat-head, round-head, or oval-head screws. To get the tightest fit possible—wood against wood—always drill a "clearance" hole in the leading piece.
- *Glue.* When used properly glue is a powerful ally of nails and screws. White glue is preferable because it doesn't require heavy clamping and is perfectly clear when dry.

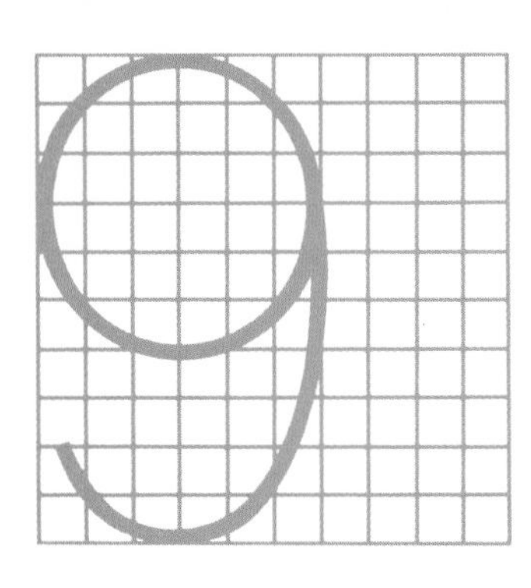

RECYCLING FURNITURE

There are lots of reasons to recycle furniture. Maybe, for budget reasons, you're faced with secondhand finds or hand-me-downs that are almost, but not quite, right. Perhaps the furnishings you've had for years are beginning to look tired—or maybe you're just tired of looking at them. Whatever stage of home decorating you're in, recycling old furniture—yours or someone else's—offers a wealth of creative, economical possibilities. The projects in this chapter tell how you can give new life to old furniture.

RE-COVERING UPHOLSTERY

Even the most durable upholstery fabric may start to show its age long before a sofa or chair exhibits any signs of structural weakness. If you have good, solid, upholstered pieces whose fabric coverings have seen better days, you *can* save them—and a lot of money in the process. An attractive new slipcover might be the answer.

Slipcovers do just what their name suggests—they cover existing upholstery. If the sofa or chair has broken springs or if its padding sticks out, new upholstery, not a slipcover, is what you need. But if the piece is still sound and you want a quick and economical surface change, consider slipcovering.

A tie-on slipcover like the one shown *at right* is easy to make. All you need are several yards of fabric, grommets, and ties or ribbon.

First, remove the loose seat cushions and measure the sofa contours from front to back and side to side, beginning and ending at the floor. Then make a drop cloth 10 inches longer and wider than the measurements.

Drape the fabric over the sofa, center it, and tuck it tightly around the seat. Next, gather in your hand the excess fabric at the corners to determine the placement of the ties. Mark the tie positions behind the folds and insert grommets at the points marked.

To hem the cover, trim the fabric 1 inch longer than the length you want. Roll the extra inch of fabric under twice and machine-stitch the hem. Slipcover the seat cushions with matching fabric and place both the finished cover and the seat cushions on the sofa. For a finishing touch, insert matching cords or ties through the grommets and secure them in a bow. *(continued)*

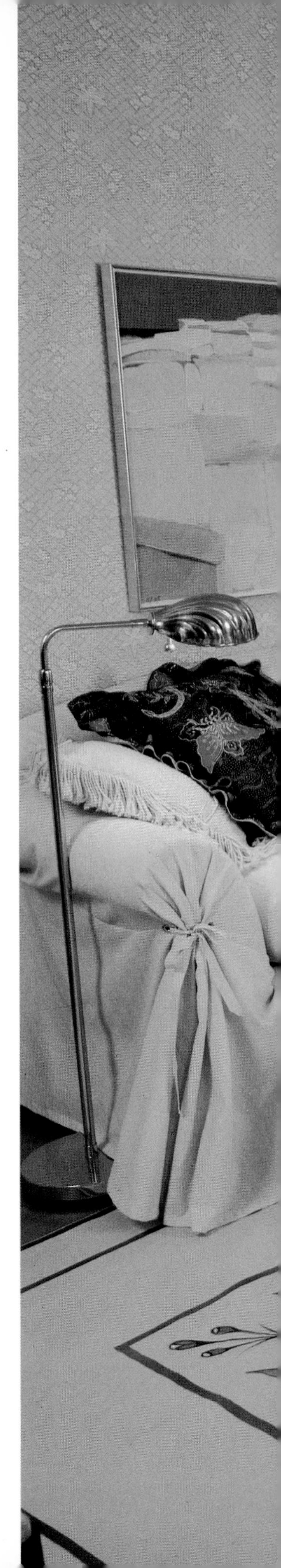

RE-COVERING UPHOLSTERY
(continued)

How much you spend for slipcovers depends on whether you choose ready-made or custom-made versions, or decide to make the covers yourself.

Probably the most inexpensive choice is the do-it-yourself slipcover; its cost depends solely on the price of the fabric you select. When you're thinking about cost—whether for homemade or custom-made slipcovers—keep in mind that an average-size armchair generally requires 7 to 8 yards of fabric, a sofa from 10 to 18 yards.

Ready-made slipcovers for chairs and sofas are available through mail-order catalogs and in some department stores. Selections tend to be limited, but ready-mades are a quick, convenient, and inexpensive solution if you find a color or pattern you like.

Custom-made slipcovers, on the other hand, offer you a greater choice of fabrics, colors, and patterns. They also provide a perfect fit that ready-mades can't match. Custom-made slipcovers are more expensive than home- or ready-mades, of course, because of the skilled labor involved. Labor costs don't vary much, but what you pay for fabric will vary widely. Choosing a low-price fabric is a good way to hold down the cost of custom-mades.

Whatever kind of slipcovers you decide to get, shop around. Get recommendations from friends, check fabric quality, and ask to see examples of finished work, if possible.

Besides economy, the major advantage that slipcovers have over new upholstery is that they come off easily for laundering or dry cleaning. And if what you're after is a quick-and-easy temporary redo, or seasonal variety, slipcovering can accomplish that, too. The chair and ottoman shown here, for instance, were upholstered in the same white fabric as the sofa (see *below*). Now check the photo *at right*. A few yards of bright, floral print fabric give the ensemble an entirely new look and the room a colorful focal point. Other color accents in the room echo the vibrant flowers of the slipcover.

REUPHOLSTERING AND RESTYLING

Reupholstering usually involves more than replacing the fabric covering on a chair or sofa; it also entails stripping a piece to its frame, repairing or replacing the padding and springs, then re-covering them. Restyling goes beyond this to include reshaping the piece for a refreshingly new look.

Reupholstering and restyling furniture are highly skilled tasks best left to a professional, and the work doesn't come cheap. But once you've invested the money, your chair or sofa will be as good as new.

If you elect to reupholster, your main tasks will be to select a suitable fabric and a capable person or firm to do the work. Bear in mind that good upholstering takes time, and, because most fabrics need special ordering, you may have a long delay before the work can even begin. Costs depend largely on the fabric you select, the number of repairs needed (if any), and whether you must replace cushions or re-cover them.

With restyling, the sky is the limit in terms of both costs and, to an extent, the look you can achieve. Arms and backs can be altered, buttons added or subtracted, and cushions reshaped or refilled. The straight-lined 1950s-look Lawson sofa shown *above,* for example, now has a country look, with extra stuffing, plump cushions, and a ruffled skirt, shown *opposite*.

Bear in mind, however, that restyling usually makes sense only if the basic shape of the frame remains unchanged. For instance, rebuilding a Lawson sofa into a contemporary piece with straight sides and a back the same height would generally cost considerably more than buying a new sofa.

How far should you go?
In deciding whether an upholstered piece is worth restyling, investigate the frame. Make sure it meets the criteria of good quality explained in Chapter 5: kiln-dried hardwood, well-crafted metal, or high-impact polystyrene frames; dowel-joined wood parts; and corner blocks screwed and nailed in place. The best frames are made of ash, an extremely tough, durable wood.

High-quality springs, also discussed in Chapter 5, are equally important. They must still provide comfort and solid, resilient support. You can completely replace springs, but again, you'd be better off simply to buy a brand-new piece.

Even if the underpinnings meet these specifications, you might still decide that restyling isn't for you. Different padding can change the *contours* of a

chair or sofa, but not its basic lines—they're determined by the frame. Within the limitations of any frame, however, you can create a variety of looks.

What are your upholstery restyling options?

- One quick, easy, and moderately inexpensive alteration is to replace attached cushions with loose ones.
- *Overstuffing* a piece can recontour its back. To achieve this look, down filling is stitched into separate sleeves that are wrapped like a comforter over the back, then covered with upholstery fabric.
- *Tufting*, which accentuates a chair's seat or back with soft indentations, gives a piece a more traditional look. Buttons or tufts—small bows made of the same fabric as tufting—often are used as accents. When the back of a piece is just studded with buttons, the indentation is slight, and the buttons have little slack material around them. When the indentation is deep, rich puckers form around the tufting, and the sofa back becomes a series of hollows and poufs. Tufting is done by sewing through the filler to anchor the cover fabric. The tautness of the pull determines the depth of the dimple.
- *Channeling* is another way to change the look of an upholstered piece. A channeled sofa appears to have ribs or ridges (the ridges may be quite wide). Each channel is a down- or batting-stuffed tube completely separated from the other channels by stitching. Channeling can run vertically or horizontally and most often is used on backs or seats.

Of course, the style and scale of the arms must complement the back. If you want plump, rounded arms that suit a well-padded back, you might try a rolled arm. One style places a rounded pad over the top of a square arm. Another type brings a rounded pad down both the inside and the outside of the arm in a long, inverted horseshoe shape to which a panel is applied.

Like the arms, the seat of the piece should suit the look and proportions of the back. Cushions may be boxy or rounded, or the seat may be tufted or padded without cushions.

Don't overlook the legs. These small details can make a big difference. Square block legs can lend an Art Deco or Oriental accent to a sofa or chair. Or you can remove the legs and replace them with a recessed base that creates the illusion that the sofa is floating.

If you've restyled a sofa into a rounded, overstuffed shape, you may want to replace the legs with ball or bun feet—wooden balls attractively finished or covered with upholstery fabric.

If you don't want to change the feet, add a skirt for a new look. A tailored flounce with box pleats, inverted pleats, or simple corner pleats can soften into gathers or remain tailored for a clean-lined look.

STRIPPING FURNITURE

Whether you're inspired by a love of antiques or by a practical desire to save money, refinishing wood furniture can be a rewarding endeavor. Refinishing is often a tedious, time-consuming task; if you acquaint yourself with basic procedures, however, you'll achieve glowing results that make *you* glow with pride. Here's some information to guide you through the process.

1

2

3

Before beginning any refinishing job, make sure it's really necessary. Many pieces that look as if they need refinishing can benefit from a thorough cleaning. To find out whether this is the case, wash an inconspicuous section of the piece with paint thinner. If a white haze appears, buff it away with extra-fine steel wool, then apply several thin coats of wax. If the results are satisfactory, you will have saved yourself a good deal of hard work.

Before you decide to refinish, also examine the wood's grain. Clear finishes are meant to bring out the beauty of the wood. If the grain isn't beautiful to begin with, other finishes, such as paint, are in order.

Starting to refinish

The first step toward refinishing is to strip off the old finish. Before you begin, make sure you have all the equipment on hand.

- *Paint or varnish remover.* Removers fall into three basic categories: paste, semi-paste, and liquid remover. Use a nonflammable, nontoxic paste for indoor work.
- *Paintbrush.* Use a cheap brush with a wooden handle and natural bristles; most paint removers contain chemicals that soften plastic handles and synthetic bristles.
- *Wide-blade putty knife.* Use this to scrape away the paint or varnish residue.
- *Steel wool.* More flexible than sandpaper, steel wool smoothes the wood and also removes the old finish from turned and carved pieces.
- *Rubber gloves and goggles.* These protect your hands and eyes from strong chemicals.
- *Rags, paper towels, and tin cans.* These all are handy for cleanups.

Whatever type of remover you choose, take precautions. If you can't work outdoors, work in a well-ventilated room and take frequent fresh-air breaks. Read the label thoroughly before opening a container of remover, paint, or stain. Procedures—and hazards—vary from product to product.

Stripping and smoothing

Now you're ready to begin stripping. Brush generous amounts of remover onto the furniture, as shown *opposite, top* (1). It's unnecessary to scrub the remover into the wood; one good swipe will do.

When the old finish has softened (small bubbles will appear on the surface), use the putty knife to lift off as much as possible, as shown *opposite.* Keep the blade at a low angle to avoid scraping the wood. Clean off the residue with a pad of steel wool, lifting the pad often as you work and dipping it in water or solvent to remove the sludge. If you're using a water-soluble stripper, wash the piece of furniture with water, but don't apply water to veneered surfaces or to glued joints.

To clean turnings, make a rope out of steel wool or burlap. Dip the rope in remover and pull it back and forth over the surface of the wood, as shown *opposite, lower left* (2). For carved areas, use a wire brush with medium-size bristles. Toothbrushes work well for cleaning small crevices as shown *opposite, lower right* (3).

After stripping and cleaning the piece, you next must prepare the bare wood. Bad blemishes require extra sanding and smoothing before you apply a new finish. As you work, use progressively finer sandpaper. Start with 220-grit paper and graduate to 400-grit paper, dusting thoroughly after each sanding. In some cases you may need to fill and possibly seal the wood grain as well. The box *at right* explains these processes.

Professional stripping

Having furniture professionally stripped is easy but expensive. There are several methods.

- "Dip and strip" involves submerging the piece in a vat of remover, then hosing it with water. This method only works for items small enough to fit into a dipping vat. The remover may dissolve glue. Never have veneer or softwood pieces dipped, and be aware that dip-stripped pieces will need sanding afterward to smooth the grain.
- A similar method is to put furniture into a dishwasher-like machine that washes it first with remover, then with water. The limitations are the same as for the dip method.
- Professional hand stripping is the most expensive, but the only commercial method that is acceptable for fine or delicate furniture.

PLUGGING, FILLING, AND SEALING

After stripping wood, you may find nail holes or cracks that you need to fill and smooth before beginning to refinish. What's more, some woods, such as fir and oak, have very prominent grains; if you want a really smooth finish, you'll need to level the grain with filler. Then you may need to apply a sealer to keep the filler from bleeding through the final finish.

Perhaps the most familiar filler is the doughy, premixed kind that's commonly used to fill holes. Other fillers, sold in paste or liquid form, level the pores in open-grain wood.

If you plan to stain the wood after filling it, buy a filler tinted to match the stain you're using—or tint it yourself before applying. Otherwise, you may end up with light spots after you apply the stain; most fillers are not especially absorbent.

Follow label instructions for applying filler. Make sure you use a liberal amount of filler because it shrinks.

Sealers amount to nothing more than a clear coating that locks in the filler or stain. Thinned shellac makes an excellent sealer, as do some varnishes.

APPLYING NEW FINISHES

Applying a new finish to wood furniture can give it new life—or restore it to its former beauty. If you don't like the wood's natural color, you may choose to darken it with stain or lighten it with bleach. Or you may think the wood is almost fine as it is, and choose a simple natural finish. Paint is another option, particularly for furniture made of undistinguished wood that has no strong grain or interesting color of its own. Finishing possibilities are extensive. Use these guidelines to help you select and apply the best finish for your furniture.

Now that you've completed stripping and prepping, take a good look at the wood. What you see will determine your next step. Whatever finish you choose, work in a well-ventilated place that has a minimum of dust.

Clear finishes

Do you like the grain and color pretty much as they are? If so, a clear finish is for you.

- *Oil* gives wood a warm glow, and it's easy to apply with a cloth, as shown *opposite.* Boiled linseed oil, either undiluted or mixed with turpentine in a ratio of two parts oil to one part turpentine, is the traditional oil finish. It usually takes six to 10 applications, lots of rubbing, and up to two weeks of drying time to achieve the patina you want. Although linseed oil isn't especially durable, it's easy to touch up. Tung oil is a more durable alternative.

For faster application and drying, use a synthetic or natural resin-oil finish—such as Danish oil—which needs only two or three applications and dries in less than 12 hours. The resin penetrates the wood and hardens the grain, making a durable finish. Resin oil is also easy to touch up.

- *Varnish* can be natural or synthetic. Either kind will give you a durable finish that, depending on the product you use, is as high-gloss or as soft and satiny as you like. Varnishes are available in colored as well as clear forms.

Apply natural resin varnish carefully with a varnish brush or cheesecloth pad. It needs at least 24 hours to dry (allow at least 36 hours to dry in humid weather). Synthetic resin varnishes are similar.

Polyurethane varnish, a synthetic product, is the most durable type of varnish. It dries rapidly, so you can apply two coats in the same day.

- *Lacquer* is a fast-drying finish; it's moderately durable but doesn't resist water. You usually apply lacquer with a spray gun. Unlike other clear finishes, it doesn't require smoothing between coats.
- *Shellac* is the least expensive clear finish, but it's easily damaged by water. Usually applied with a small brush, it gives a high-gloss finish that you can dull, if you prefer, with steel wool.
- *Wax* is primarily used to protect other clear finishes, but you also can rub it on hardwoods as a primary finish.

Stain and bleach

The range of stain colors is almost limitless. Stains come in two main types: penetrating and nonpenetrating. The former consist of dye dissolved in water, oil, or alcohol; the latter are pigment mixed with oil or other clear finish. (Some nonpenetrating stains have varnish or shellac as their solvent, but they obscure the wood's grain and give a paintlike coating.)

Water-base stains can go on all types of wood. They're inexpensive but not widely available. Alcohol-base stains are best for close-grained woods. They dry quickly and are available already mixed, but they usually require a spray gun for application. (A spray gun can be tricky to use; practice the technique on scrap material.) Oil-base penetrating stains, good for coarse-grained hardwoods, are easy to use and are long lasting; you brush or wipe them on. Oil-base nonpenetrating stains can be applied to close-grained woods, but they're a surface treatment and don't take especially well on hardwoods.

If you want to bleach wood, you can use commercial wood bleach, laundry bleach, or oxalic acid. After application, use white vinegar or soap and water to neutralize the laundry bleach, or use one part ammonia to ten parts water for oxalic acid.

Paint

Perhaps the most versatile furniture finish you can choose is paint, but it isn't a finish for fine wood—it hides the grain and color. If you decide to paint, you may hide something precious beneath a coat of bright color, and stripping wood once you've painted it is hard work. Before you paint unfinished raw wood, apply a coat of primer with a brush, as shown in the inset photo *opposite* (1). Let the primer dry thoroughly, then fill in nail holes and small cracks in the wood with spackling compound. Reprime the spackled areas. Then lightly sand the entire piece (2), working with the grain. Finish by wiping the surface clean with a tack rag.

Apply the paint with long, smooth brushstrokes (3). First brush with the grain, then across it. Next, using a nearly dry brush, go over the surface with the grain. This will eliminate any excess paint that might cause runs or thick, unsightly drips.

Alkyd enamel or oil-base paint covers wood surfaces well and provides a good wear-resistant finish. Latex-base enamel dries quickly and is a good choice for large pieces of furniture that won't get much wear. It has two drawbacks, however: It doesn't cover as well as alkyd enamel and isn't as durable.

(continued)

1
2
3

APPLYING NEW FINISHES

(continued)

The Queen Anne reproductions shown *above* were purchased unfinished. To highlight the grain, each piece was rubbed with three coats of Danish oil, a "polymerizing" liquid that penetrates into wood grain, then hardens and seals the wood as it dries. An oil finish like this not only is handsome, it's also easy to maintain. If scratches occur, just lightly sand and re-oil.

As this photo illustrates, oil finishes, which are easy to apply, give you a beautiful bare-wood look. A really fine oil finish may require several applications, and needs a final coat of hard wax for added durability.

For pieces subjected to a great deal of wear, a varnish or polyurethane finish is the best finish to use. Furnishings such as the bunk beds shown *above* wear much longer if given two coats. Both finishes are available in glossy, satin, and matte finishes; you apply each of them with a brush.

Varnish is impervious to liquids but doesn't produce the same tough, strong finish that polyurethane does. Polyurethane resists even alcohol spills and, although extremely hard, will flex with the wood as it contracts or expands.

Simple furnishings like this pencil-post bed and mission-style rocking chair call for simple finishes. A one-step maple-tone stain and sealer enhanced the bed's mellow coloring. A coat of flat polyurethane applied over the stain provides protection.

The shiny white enamel chosen for the chair is both good looking and practical. Protected by the enamel finish, this chair can work just as hard on the porch as it does in the bedroom. And all that's needed to give it a new look is a coat of enamel in a different color.

Here are some clever painting techniques you can use on children's furniture—or any place where you want to be a bit whimsical. The mini-wardrobe, except for the drawers, was painted white, then "stippled" by dipping a brush in black paint and dabbing it onto the surface. The drawers were first painted red, then covered with sections of wallpaper border. A similar treatment brightens the bookcases, and a Parsons table, protected by matching red paint, became a child-size play table. The stippled cubes make durable stools and provide extra storage.

CANING

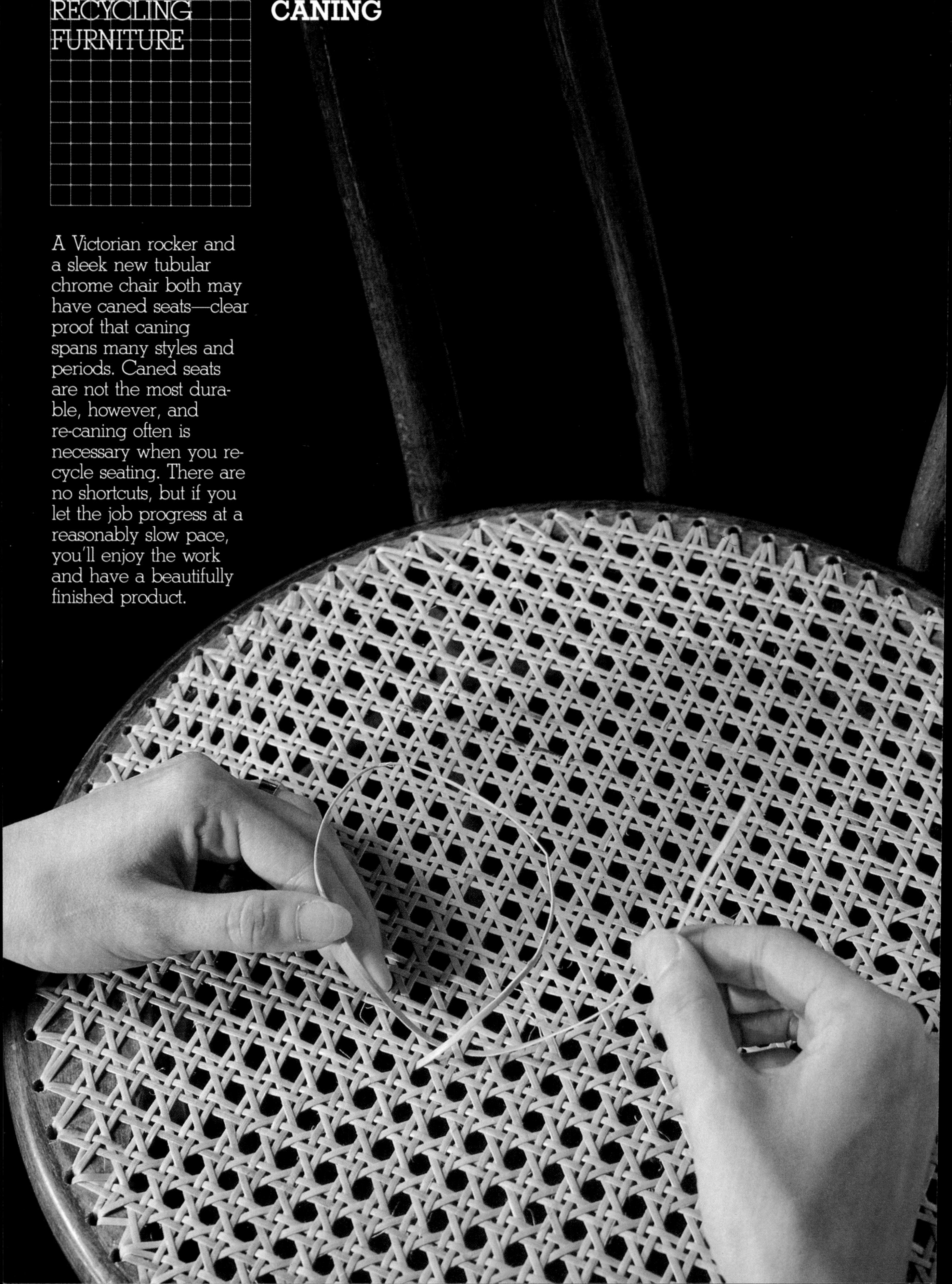

A Victorian rocker and a sleek new tubular chrome chair both may have caned seats—clear proof that caning spans many styles and periods. Caned seats are not the most durable, however, and re-caning often is necessary when you recycle seating. There are no shortcuts, but if you let the job progress at a reasonably slow pace, you'll enjoy the work and have a beautifully finished product.

To cane a chair, you need only a few tools: a caning needle, an ice pick or awl, a flat sponge, clip clothespins, and about two dozen caning pegs. The average-size chair takes about 300 feet of cane. The width of the cane you'll need varies according to the size of the holes in the chair seat and their distance apart. Here are the cane widths and hole sizes they work with.

- *Common-size cane:* 5/16-inch holes 7/8 inch apart.
- *Medium cane:* 5/16-inch holes 3/4 inch apart.
- *Fine cane:* 3/16-inch holes 5/8 inch apart.
- *Fine-fine cane:* 3/16-inch holes 1/2 inch apart.
- *Superfine cane:* 3/16-inch holes 3/8 inch apart.
- *Carriage fine cane:* 1/8-inch holes 3/8 inch apart.

Prewoven cane, or cane webbing that's loom-woven into a pattern, also is available. If your chair is made for a prewoven seat, you'll see a groove around the outside of the seat where the webbing is held in place. Then, you can simply measure the size of the seat and buy a piece of cane webbing to fit it.

If, however, the chair has holes drilled around the perimeter of the seat—indicating it was hand-caned—the seat will have to be rewoven by hand. Before starting to cane, remove the old cane and any glue or wood holding the webbing in place. Then make sure the chair is in otherwise finished form—cleaned and painted or refinished. You don't want to risk damaging the new seat.

It's also important to find a comfortable place to work. Put the chair on a table or stool so you don't have to bend over as you work.

CANING A CHAIR SEAT

Soak the cane in a tub of water so it's pliable and easy to handle.

1. Start caning at point A. Use a peg to fasten a strand in the hole. Take the strand across to point B, underneath and up through point C, then across to D, underneath and up through E, and so on. Keep the strand taut and use pegs to hold it as you work.

2. Fasten a second layer of strands at right angles over the first, using the same technique as for the first set of strands.

3. Remove pegs from the chair and fasten loose strands beneath the chair frame in knots around strands that run from hole to hole. Run the next layer of strands parallel to the first over the two previous layers.

4. Start weaving, using a caning needle. Each time you pull the strand through the hole, thread it into the needle and weave it across to the other side.

5. Arrange dampened woven strands in pairs, forcing them close together in straight, parallel lines. Weave diagonally, running two strands into each corner hole, with one hand above the chair and one beneath.

6. Weave the remaining diagonal strands from the opposite direction. As in the previous step, be sure to run two diagonals into the four corner holes. When weaving edges, be sure the strand you're weaving with is run over or under the right already-placed strands.

7. The completed caning will look like this.

1

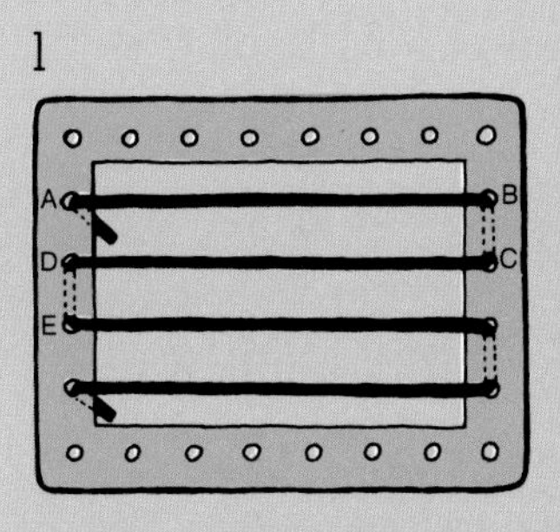

2

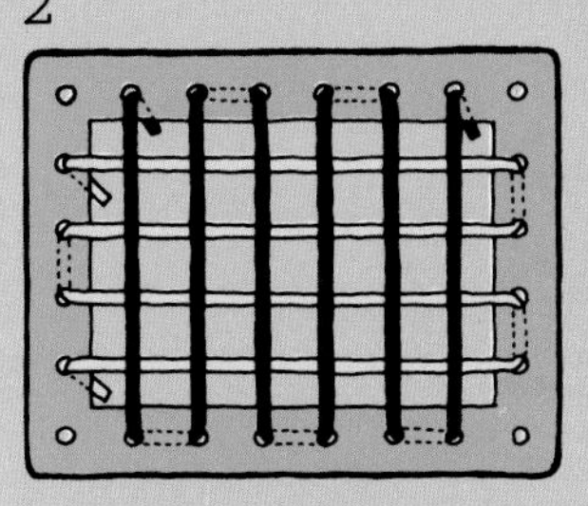

3

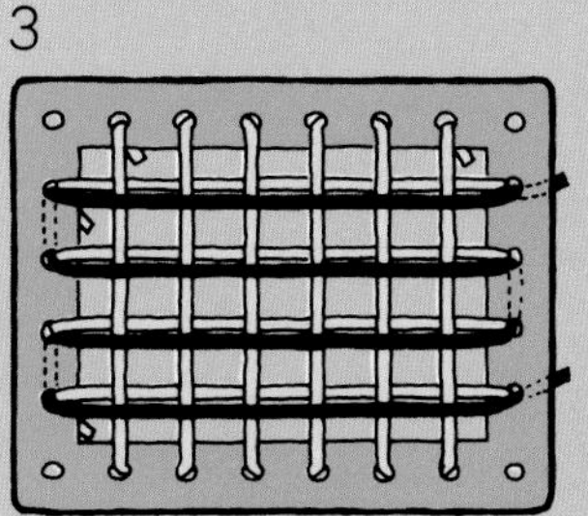

4

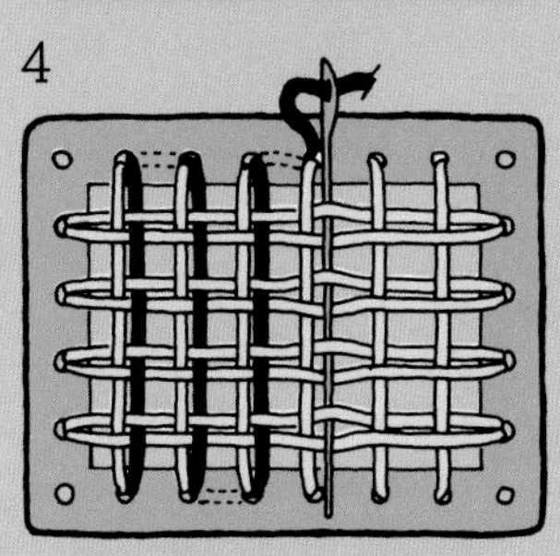

5

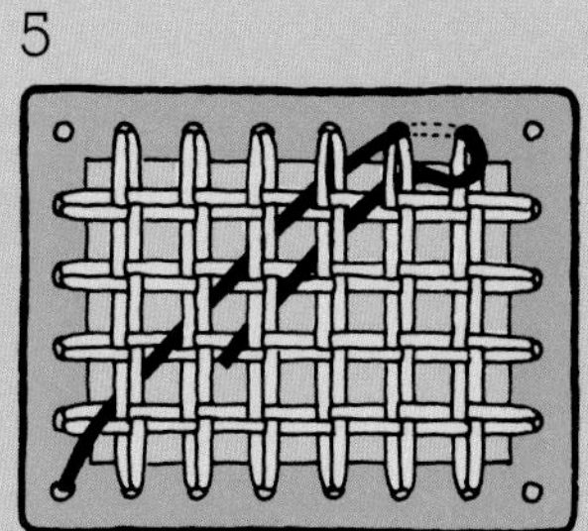

6

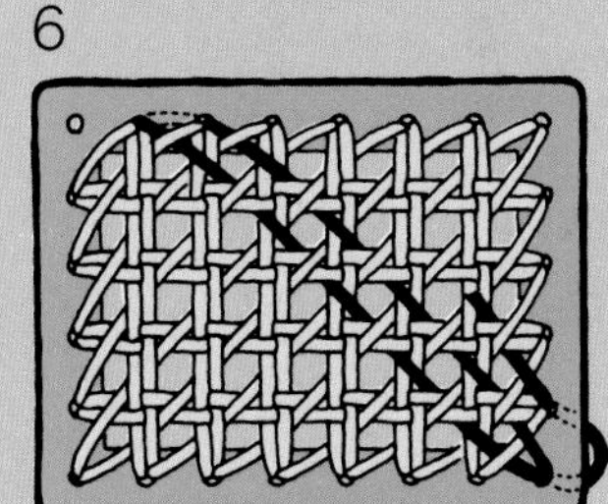

7

8

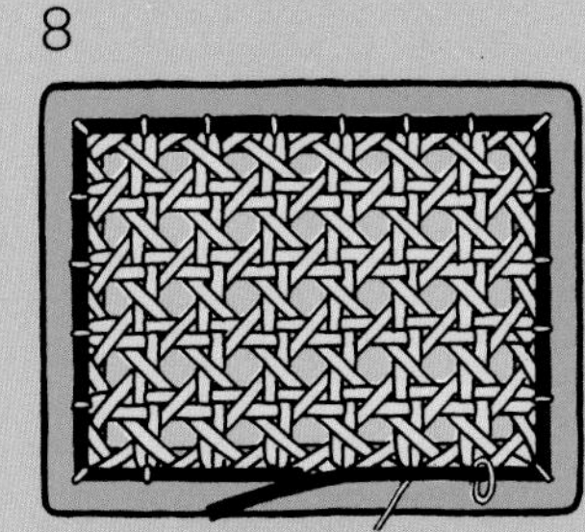

8. Using binder cane, frame the edges of woven caning. Lay binder over the holes and loop fine cane through each hole or alternate holes to secure the binder. Pull caning tightly so the binder fits snugly. To finish, lap the binder over two or three holes, fastening down these ends together. After the last loop, fasten the end of the strand by plugging the hole from beneath or tying it.

DYEING WICKER

Like fabric, wicker takes dyes well. One good reason to dye wicker rather than paint it is that dyed wicker, unlike the painted kind, doesn't peel. Because dyeing stains the wicker through and through, rather than just coating the surface, the color is much more durable. If you'd like to revive charming but shabby wicker pieces, read on.

Before you embark on a wicker-dyeing project, you should know a few of the basics.

- Wicker takes dye best if it has a dull surface; sand it lightly if you suspect the surface is too smooth.
- Unlike fabric, wicker is approximately the same color wet as it is dry.
- Excess color will rub off on clothing, so be certain to rinse the piece with clear, cold water or wipe it with a clean sponge after dyeing it. This process sets the dye and works it into the crevices.

What can you dye?

You can dye a wicker piece of any size. Tint small wicker pieces, such as baskets and serving trays, by immersing them in the dye solution in a tub or sink, as shown *above, left.* (The instructions on the dye package will tell you how to wash your sink or tub afterward to avoid staining.)

Keep the item in the dye bath for about 15 minutes or until the wicker reaches the color you want, then rinse thoroughly with cold water.

For large pieces that won't fit in the bathtub you'll have to use the sponge-on method, pictured *above, right.* Before sponge-dyeing a large item, place a plastic drop cloth beneath the piece. Then with a large sponge, wet the wicker with water. Mix the dye solution—one bottle of dye to ½ cup hot water. Sponge on the dye until the wicker is the desired shade. Allow the dye to set for 10 minutes before rinsing with cold water.

How much dye should you use?

The basic recipe for dip-dyeing is half a bottle (eight ounces) or one package of powdered dye for every three gallons of water. If you want strong, dark colors, use more dye.

Never pour dye directly on the wicker; the color will look blotchy. Instead, mix the dye thoroughly with hot water, then dip the article. Since undissolved dye particles will make small spots of intense color, dissolve powdered dye very carefully in a small container and strain it through a cloth sieve before making the solution. To avoid streaking, keep the article moving constantly through the dye.

Safety tips

As with any activity involving the use of chemicals or other potentially harmful materials, you must take safety precautions while you are working. Do not work in a food preparation area; the dyes are contaminating. Do not dye in pans you use to prepare food, and do not use aluminum, copper, or galvanized pans for dyeing projects.

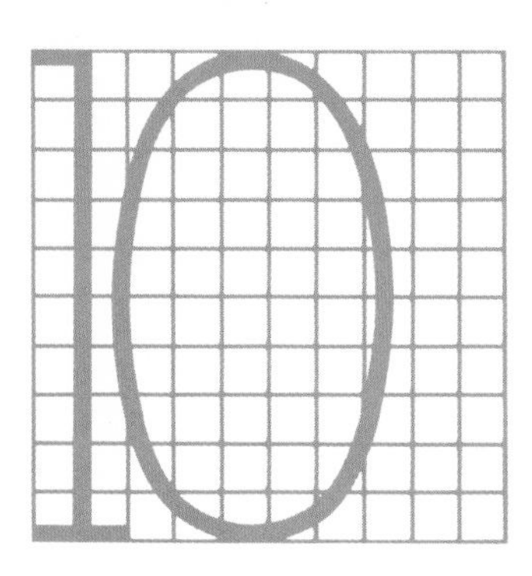

FURNITURE CARE AND REPAIR

Furniture can experience a lot of stress: careless abuse, extremes of heat and humidity, even too much attention. Wood that's too frequently cared for may become smothered by layers of old wax and polish; durable materials, such as plastic and metal, grow dull or rusty from neglect. Up to a point, you can cure or camouflage damage with some easy do-it-yourself techniques. After that, you may need to resort to a more drastic treatment. This chapter provides easy-to-follow instructions for maintaining—and, when necessary, restoring—all types of furniture.

WOOD: MAINTAINING AND REVIVING FINISHES

At its best, wood furniture is beautiful; to preserve its good looks, however, you have to take preventive measures.

Moisture and lack of moisture are the two greatest hazards wood faces. Too much humidity causes warping, mildew, and stains; too little causes shrinking that curls veneers and loosens joints. Use humidifiers or dehumidifiers to control the moisture level in your home—about 50 percent humidity is ideal.

Temperature extremes can harm wood, too. Wood furniture does best at steady temperatures of 65 to 70 degrees.

Here are some other ways to stop trouble before it starts.

- Shield wood from sunlight and from direct heat from sources such as radiators.
- Provide coasters for drinks and supply insulated pads for hot dishes.
- Dust furniture often with a soft, dry cloth.
- Protect hard finishes—varnish, shellac, lacquer, and paint—with a good carnauba paste wax. Wax isn't waterproof, but it keeps liquids from soaking into the wood quickly.
- Wax furniture only once or twice a year (two light coatings are better than one heavy coat). Occasionally wipe the waxed surface with a damp cloth to prevent soil from being ground into the wax. Buff briskly to restore the shine.
- Often wipe oil finishes clean with a soft, dry cloth; every six months wash with mild detergent and water, then re-oil. Never wax an oiled surface.

Even the best-cared-for wood furniture is bound to show some wear and tear eventually. The chart *opposite* tells how to deal with minor surface damage.

Reviving old finishes

If your wood furniture is looking generally rundown, or its surface is caked with gummy residue, something more than spot-fixing may be in order. Don't assume, however, that stripping and refinishing are the next step. If the basic finish is intact, it's better to restore it rather than risk removing the natural patina, which took years to develop.

- *Cleaning.* Museum caretakers often use a solution of mild detergent and water to remove grime from antique furniture, but you should use this cleaning method cautiously. Don't wash shellac or lacquer finishes, and never use water on veneered or inlaid pieces.

Before washing an entire piece, try the solution on a small hidden spot on the furniture. If no white bloom appears after the spot dries, wash the rest of the piece. Dip the cloth in a detergent solution, wring it as dry as possible, and wash a small area at a time. Next wipe with a cloth wrung out in clear warm water. Dry the wood with a clean cloth.

- *Reconditioning.* Several commercial refinishers (not strippers or removers) for reconditioning varnish, shellac, or lacquer are available in paint departments. They're expensive but effective and easy to use. Often referred to as *amalgamators,* they remove all the old wax, polishes, dirt, discolorations, and top layers of finish, then liquefy the remaining clean finish so it melts into cracks and scratches and hardens into a smooth surface. The original wood filler, sealer, and stain remain intact. Refinishers are not strong enough to work on paint, epoxy, or polyurethane varnish, and shouldn't be used on oil finishes. (For refinishers you can make, see the box *opposite.*)

HOW TO MAKE A CLEANER/ REFINISHER

First, identify the finish on a furniture piece by moistening one spot with denatured alcohol, another with lacquer thinner. If the alcohol spot softens, the finish is shellac. If the lacquer-thinner spot softens, the finish is lacquer. If neither softens, the finish is varnish. (To test for an oil finish, use turpentine as a solvent.)

- Clean and soften old *varnish* with a heated solution of one part turpentine and three parts boiled linseed oil. (Heat in an uncovered container of hot water, not over an open flame.) Rub on with a soft cloth; wipe with a cloth wrung out in warm water. For heavy soil, use more turpentine and rub with super-fine steel wool.
- To liquefy old *lacquer* into a smooth surface, apply lacquer thinner, brushing first across, then with the grain. For deep damage, repeat.
- Soften *shellac* or *polyurethane* by rubbing firmly with steel wool dipped into a paste of pumice and linseed oil. Clean with a turpentine-dampened cloth.
- Remove stains on an *oil* finish with turpentine, then apply a solution of equal parts turpentine and boiled linseed oil. Let soak in for 15 minutes; wipe off residue.

REPAIRING MINOR FINISH DAMAGE

SCRATCHES

Home remedies. For a scratch on an oil finish, rub with linseed oil and wipe dry. On varnish or shellac use paste shoe polish that matches the finish. Rub walnut furniture with the meat of a Brazil nut or black walnut. Apply fresh iodine to red mahogany, aged brown iodine to brown mahogany. For maple, dilute iodine with denatured alcohol until it's the right color.
Commercial remedies. Wax sticks, available at paint and hardware stores in a variety of shades, hide minor scratches. For a wider or deeper scratch, first clean out the scratch with extra-fine sandpaper, then apply an oil stain with a cotton swab. Let the stain dry and fill the crack with coats of clear nail polish until the filler is level with the surrounding surface. Shellac sticks also are good for filling wide cracks. Follow the manufacturer's instructions.

CHECKING OR CRAZING

Cause. Too much sun can cause dozens of tiny hairline cracks on varnish or shellac finishes.
Cure. If the crazed area is large, try melding the cracks together with a refinisher. If the area is small, rub the damaged section with fine steel wool dipped in paste wax. If these remedies don't work, the furniture needs stripping and refinishing to regain its smooth finish.

CLOUDY FINISH

Cause. High humidity can dull waxed surfaces.
Cure. Clean with naphtha or mineral spirits to dissolve the wax, so you can wipe away the cloudy part.

WHITE RINGS AND MARKS

Cause. Water, alcohol, excessive heat from dishes or pans.
Cure. Remove water rings by rubbing with toothpaste on a soft rag, or with oil mixed with a mild abrasive such as cigarette ashes, salt, or rottenstone. Remove alcohol spots by rubbing lightly with a rag dipped in ammonia. To remove heat blemishes, dampen the area with camphorated oil. Wipe and let dry, then rub with rottenstone and oil. Buff the surface smooth with furniture polish or oil after a stain is removed.

BLACK RINGS OR SPOTS

Cause. Standing water from plants or pets.
Cure. These are hard to remove and are best left to professionals.

BURNS

Dissolve a superficial scorch by rubbing with a little nail polish remover on the tip of a cotton swab. Use a razor blade to remove the charred wood; clean the area with naphtha. Then repair as you would a deep scratch.

PAINT SPOTS

Use fine steel wool dipped in liquid wax to rub away alkyd paint that is still damp. Fresh water-base paint can be removed with a damp cloth. Wipe away dried paint (alkyd or latex) with boiled linseed oil. If that doesn't work, apply a paste of rottenstone and boiled linseed oil, let dry, and wipe off. On lacquer finish, apply a drop of nail polish remover on a cotton swab, being careful not to touch the surrounding finish. Let the remover work a few seconds, then rub the spot off with a little toothpaste on a cloth.

REPAIRING WOOD FURNITURE

SOLVING COMMON SURFACE PROBLEMS

REPAIRING BUBBLED OR BLISTERED VENEER

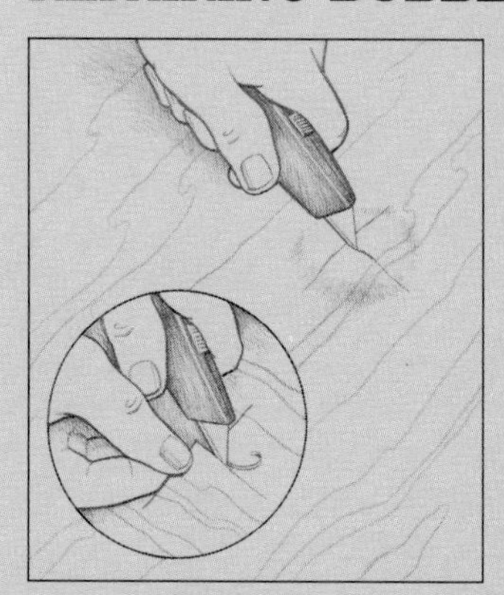

1 A bubble or blister in the wood means glue beneath the veneer has separated or dried out. Using a sharp knife, make a cut in the blister's center, cutting with the wood grain. Make a second cut at right angles. Lift the flaps carefully; using a damp cotton swab, clean away the old glue. Shave a tiny slice off half of the cut. Press the blister flat.Trim until edges fit.

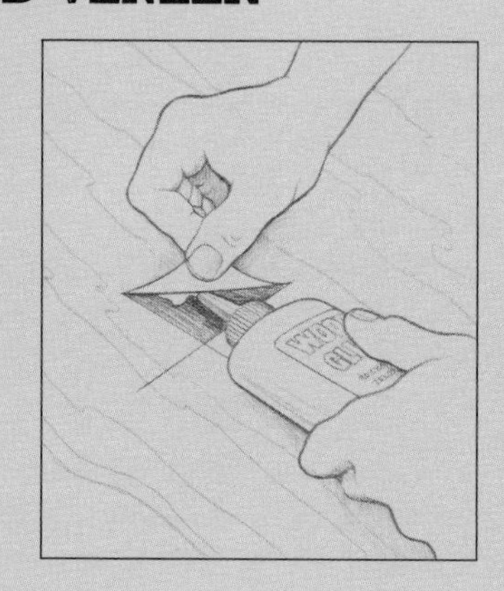

2 When wood that has bubbled up can be pressed flat and tight, squirt glue under the flaps and press the edges together. Wipe up any glue that oozes out. Spread waxed paper over the glued spot and weight the area with a stack of books. If a crack shows after the glue dries, fill with stick shellac. Refinish the area, if necessary.

REPAIRING DENTS IN SOLID WOOD

1 A shallow dent that hasn't broken the wood fibers often can be raised with steam heat. Steam damages the finish, however, so you'll need to refinish the repaired area. First, scrape the surface free of finish. Then apply heat with a fairly hot iron (separated from the wood by layers of wet cloth). You may have to rewet the cloth pad and repeat the process.

2 For small, deep dents, put a small pad of wet cloth over the dent, and place a metal bottle cap, hollow side down, over the pad. Hold a soldering iron to the cap. Repeat as needed. For large, deep dents, use a sheet of aluminum. Place the sheet over a large wet pad and apply heat with a propane torch. Keep the torch in constant motion over the sheet.

Veneer may pose a special problem for you. It can come loose around the edges, or a section may chip and need replacing.

If you catch a simple loose edge early—before dirt seeps under the veneer—regluing and weighting the area may solve the problem.

If dirt has gotten under the veneer, you may have to cut out a flap in order to scrape out the dirt and old glue. Soften old glue with vinegar or with a special solvent available at lumberyards and paint stores. Using a putty knife, force new glue between the underlay and the veneer. Press surfaces together and wipe away excess glue. Clamp the edges together until the glue dries.

To replace a piece of veneer that has broken off, you have to find a matching piece—and that's a challenge. You may be able to get small sheets of veneer from a hardwoods dealer or furniture maker.

Chisel cut out the damaged veneer and scrape out old veneer fibers and glue. If a few spots need patching, replace an entire section rather than make several small patches.

Make a paper pattern of the hole, using tracing paper. To make a patch, cut out a piece of new veneer approximately the same size as the damaged area. Put it over the hole and shift it until it matches the surrounding grain as closely as possible. Then, using a veneer saw or sharp knife, cut the veneer exactly to shape according to the pattern.

Fit the patch into the hole (do not glue yet). You may have to sand or file off the edges to get a perfect fit. Sand the surface of the patch to bring it level with the surrounding area. Remove the patch.

Apply glue to the underlay. Press the patch firmly into place. Wipe off excess glue, then clamp or weight the mended area.

REPAIRING WOBBLY FRAMES

TIGHTENING A LOOSE STRETCHER

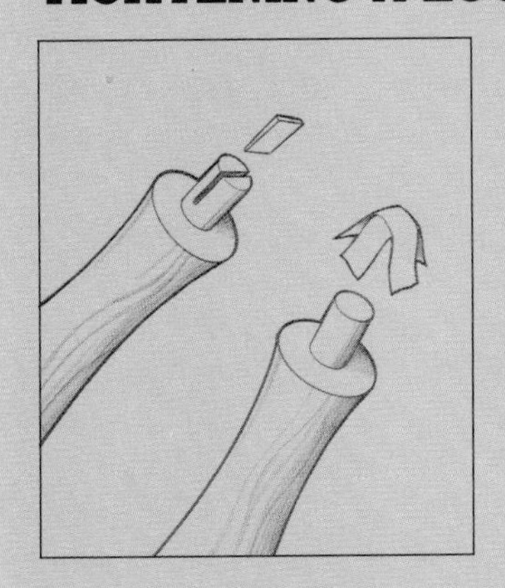

1 To fix a loose stretcher, first spread apart the chair legs so you can get the end of the rung out of the hole. Be careful not to loosen the other joints. If the rung is too small, expand its end by cutting a slot across it and inserting a wedge. If the rung is only a little loose, wrap thread or fabric around it, gluing it in place. Let dry before refitting the rung.

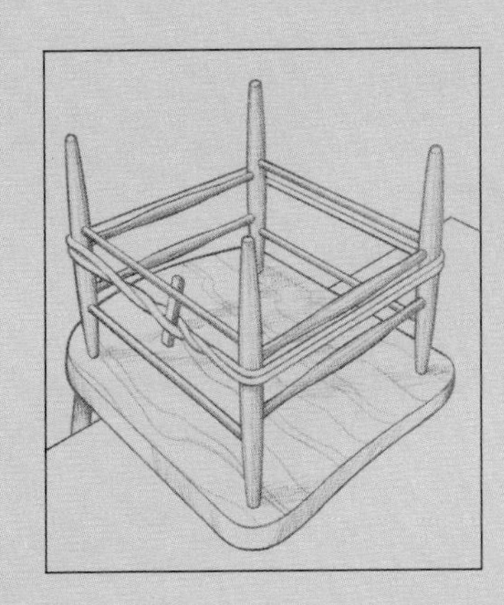

2 Clean out the hole. Dissolve old glue with hot vinegar, and scrape it out. Apply glue to the hole and push the rung into place. Use a band clamp or a length of rope to hold the mended sections together. Wrap the rope around the legs in double strands and insert a stick, tourniquet-style, to tighten the rope.

REPAIRING BROKEN JOINTS WITH DOWELS

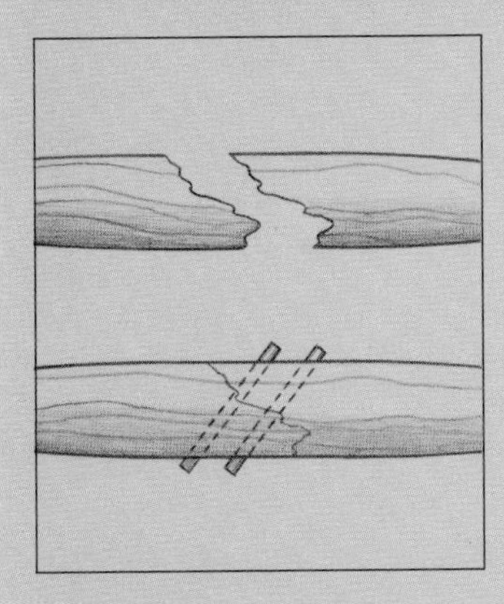

1 You can mend broken legs, stretchers, or rungs if the break is clean and the sections fit together neatly. First, clamp broken parts together without gluing. Drill, at an angle, holes for dowels through both sections. Glue the broken parts together. Insert dowels and tap them into place using a mallet. Clamp the parts together until the glue dries.

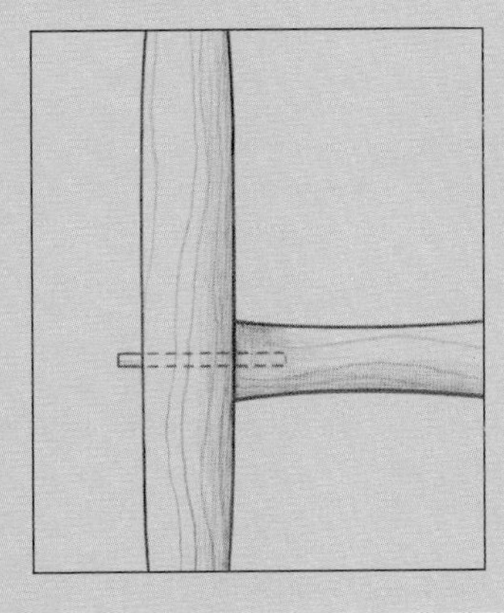

2 You can use dowels without screws to strengthen and secure a joint in a chair rung where a screw will not fit. Drill holes with a bit the same diameter as the dowel you plan to use. Cut spiral grooves in the dowels to hold glue. Use plenty of glue on the dowels and in the holes. Clamp until the glue is dry, then trim the dowels and refinish.

ADDING NEW CORNER WEDGES

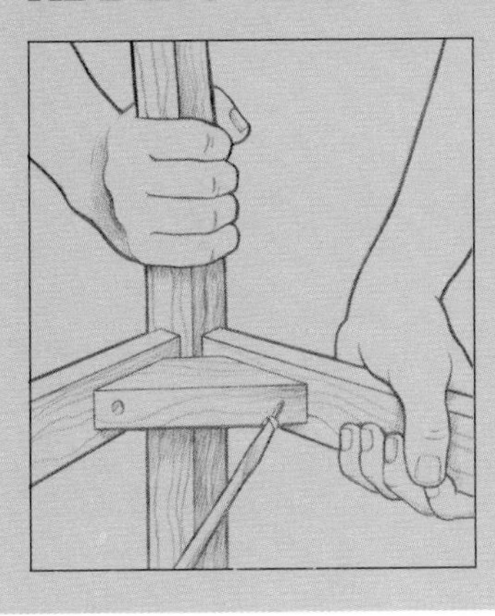

1 When repairing the frame of an upholstered chair, you may find that the manufacturer failed to install corner wedges to reinforce joints and help make the chairs more rigid. If so, be sure to add them. To do so, cut blocks from hardwood, and fit them tightly into a corner. Then glue them into place. Attach screws through each block and into a rail on each side.

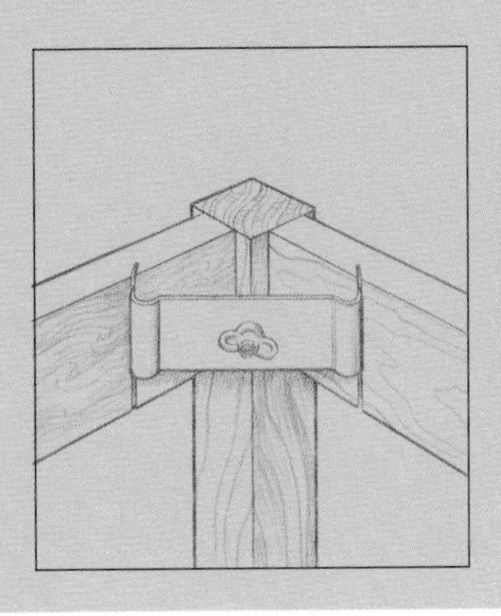

2 Check your dining table to see whether it has corner wedges, metal brackets, or other devices between the tabletop and top of each leg. Wood wedges should always be both glued and screwed for better bracing. If the table has no support devices, add corner blocks as for chairs.

CARING FOR UPHOLSTERY

Like wood furniture, upholstered pieces thrive in moderate temperatures and moderate humidity. Also like wood furniture, they suffer damage from direct heat and sunlight, dust, and excess moisture. Regular vacuuming is the key to preserving upholstered furniture's fresh look.

Most upholstery fabrics can be safely cleaned without professional help, but some manufacturers advise professional cleaning for certain materials—rayon and some of the new silks, for example. Use the chart *opposite* as a guide, and check the item for attached care instructions.

General cleaning

The time to clean your upholstered furniture is before it looks badly soiled. A gray tint or darkening around the arms or headrest means it's almost past time for a thorough cleaning. Before you clean a fabric, test it for shrinkage and color fastness this way:

- Sponge an inconspicuous spot with the cleaning solution you plan to use—either a commercial upholstery shampoo or a homemade solution of a half-cup laundry detergent to a gallon of water. Let the fabric dry. Shrinkage will be obvious.
- Test for color fastness by pressing a white paper towel dampened with the cleaning solution against the fabric, again in an inconspicuous spot. If it leaves a stain, the color will run, and you should use a dry-cleaning solvent.

To make your own shampoo, whip a mild detergent and water to a dry foam—it's the lather, not the liquid, you want to apply. Brush on the foam with a sponge, working quickly and scrubbing a small area at a time. Use a circular motion on loop fabrics and flat, straight strokes on cut-pile fabrics. Lift off the dirty foam with a clean towel, then rinse the area with a clean cloth dipped in warm water and wrung almost dry. Go on to the next area.

For machine cleaning of waterproof fabrics, rent a water-extraction carpet-cleaning machine with an upholstery attachment. The manufacturers of these machines usually recommend specific cleaning products. They also provide instructions.

To clean fabrics that are not colorfast or shrinkproof, sponge with a dry-cleaning solvent. Use the solvent sparingly, and wipe it off before it soaks into the filling; otherwise, it may damage foam rubber and polyurethane.

Dry upholstery as quickly as possible in the draft of a fan. Don't use a hair dryer or other source of heat for solvent-treated upholstery: The solvents are often flammable.

Protective finishes

Most upholstery fabrics are factory-treated with a soil and stain repellent such as Scotchgard or Teflon, which makes them easier to clean. Generally, you can clean a fabric two or three times before you need to renew the factory-applied finish. Spray-on fabric protectors are available at supermarkets and at home-center stores.

Treating spots

Spills and spots are almost inevitable. To keep them from becoming permanent stains, you need to work fast.

- Immediately blot up spilled liquids with a clean cloth or white paper towel. Never rub the spill—rubbing forces the residue into the fabric's fibers. Remove any solid substances with a spatula.
- If the fabric isn't harmed by water, sponge the area with a little clear water and blot it up. Then treat with either a detergent solution or a solvent, depending on the type of stain. There are two main types of stains—*oil-based* and *water-based.* Water-based stains include beer, soft drinks, toothpaste, mustard, and white shoe polish. If the fabric is colorfast and won't be damaged by water, use detergent and water on this type of stain.

Oil-based stains include almost anything greasy, from butter to wax. For these, a dry-cleaning solvent or spot remover is the best hope. Some stains—such as peanut butter, salad dressing, ice cream, and coffee and tea with milk or cream—are a combination of the two types. Use a solvent first, then a detergent.

- For spot-treating new stains, you usually can use a dry-cleaning solvent full-strength from its container.
- To make a spot-treating detergent solution, mix one cup of mild detergent with a gallon of water.
- For a mild bleaching solution, add a teaspooon of ammonia or white vinegar to a quart of cool water.

Use only as much stain remover as necessary. Using a barely damp cloth pad, whisk it across the stain lightly so the fabric will absorb the solution slowly. Try to keep the wet area from spreading. If the stain still remains, use a little more cleaning solution on the pad. Dab around the edges of the stain, working toward the center. Change the cleaning pad often to avoid redepositing the stain. Pat and blot with a dry cloth. You will probably have to repeat the treatment several times.

SPECIAL STAINS

- *Ball-point pen.* Apply a few drops of lukewarm glycerine to the spot and let it soak in for a few minutes. When the stain loosens, blot it up.
- *Mildew.* If the fabric is colorfast, apply diluted household bleach (one teaspoon bleach to one tablespoon water), let the bleach remain for no more than two minutes, then wash with detergent solution. If the fabric is not washable, use hydrogen peroxide instead of ammonia and detergent.
- *Soft drinks.* Clean spots immediately with detergent solution.

TYPES OF FABRICS

	REGULAR AND SPECIAL CARE	SPOT AND STAIN REMOVAL
COTTON	Vacuum weekly. Keep upholstery dry; cotton is susceptible to mildew—a fungus that thrives on damp cloth—and untreated cotton dries slowly. Protect fabric from direct light to avoid fading, and turn cushions to distribute wear.	Soak up spills as they occur. Do not use hot water—it will set stains. Sponge oily stains with cleaning fluid or a powder cleaner that absorbs grease. If possible, put a blotter or cloth under the fabric when you clean it.
LINEN	Brush or vacuum regularly.	Use cool water and a small amount of upholstery cleaner on non-oily stains. Remove oily ones with cleaning solvent. Don't bleach—it will weaken fibers and may leave its own stain.
WOOL	Use a natural-bristle brush or a lint remover before vacuuming: Vacuuming won't remove lint, threads, or pet hairs. Treat with moth repellent for longer wear.	Some wool is washable, but most should be dry-cleaned. Consult the manufacturer's instructions. Sponge stains with cool water, using upholstery cleaner if necessary. Bleach will damage fibers. Do not dry wool with direct heat; it will turn the fibers brittle. Rust and ink stains need professional treatment.
SYNTHETICS	Regular vacuuming will remove surface dust and soil. For blends of synthetic fibers, follow the cleaning procedure for the fiber that needs the most careful treatment.	Almost any spill will wash off stain-resistant *olefin.* Remove non-oily stains from *polyester* with clear, warm water. Solvent may damage *acrylic,* but non-greasy stains respond to warm water. *Nylon* resists non-oily stains, but oily stains must be spot-cleaned quickly. *Rayon* usually needs dry cleaning.
LEATHER	Dusting and an occasional sudsing may be sufficient for new leather, which usually has a special finish to prevent drying and cracking. Old leather needs an occasional dressing with leather cream or saddle soap. Never use plastic covers over leather. Brush suede by hand or vacuum with a soft brush attachment.	Some old leather can't tolerate water, so clean stains with a 60-40 blend of lanolin and neat's-foot oil. Use a special cleaning compound for stains on suede. Heavily stained suede or smooth leather will need professional cleaning. Do not use surface-protecting spray on suede or leather.
LEATHER-LIKE VINYL	Dust to remove surface soil. Wipe regularly with a damp cloth. Never use dry-cleaning solvents, scouring powder, or any ammonia product. Apply paste wax to protect areas that are subject to staining, and buff well.	Sponge off heavy soil with warm water and a mild detergent, or a special vinyl cleaner-conditioner. Let the cleaner stand for a few minutes to loosen dirt, then wipe away with a clean damp cloth. Use alcohol to remove marks from ball-point pens; rinse with clear water.

CARING FOR SPECIAL MATERIALS

MAINTAINING AND RENEWING SPECIAL MATERIALS

ACRYLICS

Better known by brand names such as Lucite and Plexiglas, acrylic plastics are used for tabletops and occasional pieces.

- Acrylic surfaces attract dust, so wipe them frequently with a chamois. Go over surfaces with a clean damp cloth to minimize static electricity. Shine with an ammonia-and-water solution. If the surface is extra dirty, rub it with a sponge dipped in a mild detergent and water mixture. Rinse well and blot dry with a soft cloth or chamois.
- Acrylic is almost unbreakable, but it scratches easily. Rub away shallow scratches with toothpaste or paste wax, applied on a soft cloth. Buff with a cotton flannel rag. Sand deeper scratches with very fine sandpaper and buff with a fine-grit compound. After the scratches are erased, apply a coat of automobile paste wax to protect the surface.
- To remove paint or heavy grease spots, use kerosene. Never use scouring powder or strong solvents.

While acrylics are impervious to kerosene or naphtha, they can be harmed by other chemicals. Gasoline, alcohol, benzine, acetone, lacquer thinners, dry cleaning fluids, and many window cleaning spray compounds can cloud and roughen acrylic surfaces.

BRASS

Brass is actually an alloy. The solid brass used for high-quality beds or table or chair frames is 70 percent copper and 30 percent zinc. On less expensive furniture, brass is applied in a thin coat (plating) over other metal.

- Most new brass furniture, whether solid or plated, has a clear, baked-on lacquer coating that protects the shine. Dust and wash occasionally with a damp cloth to keep the metal gleaming. If the lacquer film is scratched or cracked, however, the exposed area will begin to tarnish and the item will have to be professionally relacquered.
- Old brass pieces are unlikely to have a lacquer coat; clean them with special brass polish. (You can have old brass lacquered to protect it. Many people, however, prefer to retain the authentic unlacquered finish. In any case, don't lacquer brass pieces, such as andirons, that may come in contact with an open fire.) If unlacquered brass has tarnish spots on it, buff them away with an electric buffer; or use a brass cleaner to remove the tarnish. If your old brass is a treasured antique, don't rub too hard, or you will rub away the patina.
- Do not use the old-time vinegar-and-salt treatment on brass. Any trace of it left unremoved will damage the metal. Also avoid steel wool and cutting abrasives.

BUTCHER BLOCK

True butcher block is made of strips or blocks of wood, usually maple, glued together so the edge grain is on top.

- Oil a new piece often for the first several months, and every two or three months thereafter. Oil the undersides occasionally—two or three times a year is enough. Rub on the oil with a pad of cheesecloth that has been washed to remove the sizing. Let the oil soak in for an hour, then remove the residue with an old soft terrycloth towel. Polish the surface briskly.
- If you prepare food on your butcher block, rub the surface with mineral oil or vegetable oil. Otherwise, use linseed oil.
- Clean a tabletop after each use with a dry cloth or one dampened with a little oil.
- Remove stains and scratches with sandpaper. Use coarse sandpaper for hard rock maple, finer grades on other woods. Re-oil after sanding.
- Some butcher block has a polyurethane coating and wipes clean with a damp cloth. Rub scratches out of polyurethane with furniture polish. Although coated butcher block won't dry out as fast as untreated wood, it does need an occasional oiling.

CHROME

Good chrome plating lasts almost forever without rusting or corroding, but lower-priced chrome can be vulnerable to salt spray and rugged use.

- For regular cleaning, wipe chrome with rubbing alcohol. Rub alcohol on with a soft cloth and buff until any water spots are removed. If the metal is especially dirty, wash it with detergent and water. Follow with an automobile chrome cleaner; the detergent will leave streaks.
- To keep scratches from rusting, spray them with automobile chrome protector. The protector doesn't last long out-of-doors, so several applications a year are necessary if your furniture is exposed to the weather. If rust has started, remove it by scraping along the rusty scratch with the point of a toothpick dipped in penetrating oil. Be sure the oil doesn't drip onto other parts of the piece. After the rust is removed, clean the surface and spray on the protector.

MARBLE

Marble mars surprisingly easily and needs special care to look its best.

• Dust with a soft brush; cloth may grind dirt into the surface and dull the marble.

• Wash frequently with clear, warm water; once or twice a year, add mild detergent to the water. Work in small sections and rinse with clear water. Dry with a chamois.

• Apply a protective coat of marble polish or wax.

• To remove a stain, wash the area with hydrogen peroxide mixed with a few drops of ammonia. Rinse well. To remove deep stains, try an absorbent poultice: for organic stains, a paste of whiting (available at paint stores) and peroxide; for grease stains, peroxide and benzene. Spread over the stain and cover with a damp cloth. After drawing out the stain, wash with mild detergent, rinse, and buff dry.

Marble cleaning kits also are available from some manufacturers. They can be used to remove dirt, dust, smoke and other surface stains.

Many antique marble statues darken and weather with age. In most cases, this patina is favorable and if removed, can decrease the piece's market value.

NONPLASTIC LAMINATES

A great many products, including fabric, mirrors, rattan, even leather, are laminated to furniture; most are protected by a lacquered or durable plastic finish.

• Clean fabric laminates with a general household spray cleaner, brushing it into very soiled areas in a circular motion. Blot with a damp absorbent cloth and rinse thoroughly.

• Clean metallic laminate with mild detergent and water. Never use a solvent or general-purpose cleaner on metallics.

• Laminated mirror surfaces should be cleaned with commercial glass cleaner or with a warm water and ammonia solution. Spray the cleaner onto a soft cloth, then wipe the mirror. Be sure the solution doesn't drip around the edges of the mirror or the silver backing may be harmed.

• Wash other laminates with mild detergent or with household spray cleaners.

• Remove stains with a paste of baking soda and water. Let the paste stand a minute or two, then blot away. Denatured alcohol may help if used carefully; chlorine bleach is a last resort. Do not use abrasives or cleaning powders. Pretest laminated surfaces before you use any product.

PLASTIC LAMINATE

Originally designed for kitchen counter tops, plastic laminate is easy to care for, very durable, and resistant to heat, stains, moisture, and grease—but it can be damaged by sharp knives, cigarette and other burns, and nail polish, for example. Most of these ills cannot be cured except by cutting out and replacing the damaged section.

• Wash plastic with a mild liquid detergent and water solution. Rinse and dry with a soft cloth. If necessary, scrub plastic with a brush or plastic pot scrubber, but avoid abrasive cleaners, which will dull the surface. Also don't use cleaners with ammonia or those labeled "not safe for plastics." For best results, use cleaners specially made for laminated plastics. These cleaners leave an antistatic finish that repels dirt.

• For extra protection, polish a matte finish with cream wax.

• Use liquid wax on a high-gloss finish.

• Try to remove stains with a damp paste of water and baking soda. This will usually lift the stain quickly. If not, dampen a cloth with household bleach and rinse immediately with clean water.

POLYESTER RESIN

A polyester-resin finish looks like lacquer but is less fragile. This high-gloss, luxurious-looking surface is made of a shiny synthetic coating over a lacquer base. It doesn't smudge or soil easily but needs regular cleaning and buffing to maintain its glamorous high gloss.

Treat polyester resin as you would any other fine furniture surface. Protect it from extremes of heat and humidity.

• Clean with a good window-glass cleaner or a solution of ammonia and water. Two tablespoons of ammonia to a quart of water will clean off even stubborn grime. Dip a soft cloth in a warm solution, wring it out, and rub it over the surface. Wipe with a cloth dipped in clear water and buff dry with a soft cloth. Don't use spray can polishes that contain silicone. These can leave a shiny, sticky coating on a synthetic finish.

• Remove scratches with a good automobile wax. Rub the wax into the scratch with a cotton swab and polish with a soft cloth.

Polyester resin finishes can be damaged by extreme heat and humidity. Keep furniture out of direct sunlight and don't place it close to hot or cold air ducts or a fireplace.

A GLOSSARY OF FURNITURE TERMS

Acanthus. Design motif that resembles the thick, thistlelike leaves of acanthus plant; used to decorate traditional furniture moldings, legs, and arms.
Acetate. Manufactured fiber made by treating cellulose with chemicals; used in upholstery fabrics.
Adaptation. Newly made furniture piece largely patterned after an old, and often classic, item.
Angle iron. Steel fastener with an L-shape cross-section; used to join structural parts of furniture.
Antique. In general terms, a work of art, piece of furniture, or decorative object that's at least 100 years old.
Apron. On a chair or table, a decorative panel that runs from leg to leg below the seat or tabletop; in a window, the horizontal molding below the sill.
Armoire. Originally a French term for a cabinet used to store armor, now usually a tall wardrobe with doors.
Balance. Decoratively, an element resulting from an arrangement that revolves around an imaginary central point and that maintains a pleasant sense of being evenly weighted on each side. In symmetrical balance, like objects are mirrored on both sides of the central point; asymmetrical balance uses unlike, but evenly weighted, objects.
Ball foot. Ball-shaped foot used in early design periods.
Baluster. Vertical support for a rail, chair, or table, often shaped like a vase.
Banister. Upright, usually slender, support for a handrail in a stairway.
Banquette. French term for a long, upholstered seat or bench, often built in.
Barcelona chair. Twentieth-century chair designed by Ludwig Mies van der Rohe; made of stainless steel, with legs that cross beneath the seat to form the back and seat supports.
Bauhaus. A German school founded in 1919 for the study of art, industrial design, and architecture; noted for its influence in modern designs that incorporated new technology with functional beauty.
Bentwood. Steam-softened wood molded into furniture parts, most notably chair backs, seats, and arms.
Bérgère. Armchair with closed upholstered sides, high back, and loose seat cushion, first made during Louis XV period.
Bevel. An angle formed with two surfaces that meet but are not at a right angle; also an edge cut at a slant to the main surface.
Bird's-eye. Mottled pattern in wood that suggests a bird's eye, most common in maple, birch, and white ash.
Bolster. Long, round, square, or oval cushion often used as a back rest for banquettes.
Bombé. The bulging front or sides of a chest, most often seen on cabinetry pieces from the French Louis XV and rococo periods.
Bonnet top. A rounded, curved or scrolled raised top on seventeenth- and eighteenth-century American highboys and secretaries.
Bow front. The front of a case piece that has an outward curve, popular in eighteenth-century English designs.
Bracket foot. Common style of furniture support in eighteenth-century designs, shaped like an L bracket and often splayed or curved.
Breakfront. A high, wide cabinet with a projecting center section; the top section is often glazed.
Brocade. A formal fabric with a raised, embroiderylike pattern; heavy weights of it are often used for upholstery.
Broken pediment. A pediment with open center space for a decorative urn or finial.
Bull's-eye mirror. A decorative round mirror with convex or concave glass.
Bureau. A chest of drawers, often topped by a mirror.
Burl. Wood cut from a domelike growth on a tree, often strongly marked and saved for exquisite veneers.
Butler's tray. A large serving tray with hinged sides, often placed on a stand with legs to form a low table.
Cabriole. A decorative chair or table leg that curves outward at the knee, then tapers in at the ankle, and ends in a scroll at the foot to make an S shape.
Camelback. A back with the top rail curved up in the center.
Campaign furniture. Furniture fashioned after pieces used on military campaigns; distinctive for its metal-trimmed corners and recessed hardware.
Cane. Slender woody stems used for frames in casual furniture, or split into strands and woven around joints or into backs and seats.
Chaise longue. A chair with an elongated seat for sitting with legs outstretched.
Channel back. An upholstered back with rows of vertical tufting.
Cheval glass. A long, pivoting mirror hung between two posts.
Chinoiserie. Elaborate and intricate decoration on furniture inspired by Chinese art and often painted or lacquered.
Chintz. A lightweight, glazed-cotton cloth that frequently features large-scale floral patterns; commonly used for slipcovers and light draperies.
Claw-and-ball foot. The end of a chair or table leg that resembles an animal's paw—such as that of a lion—grasping a ball.
Club foot. A thick, slightly curved foot often used on eighteenth-century furniture.
Comb back. A Windsor chair-back in which the central group of spindles extends above the back and is topped with an additional rail, resembling an old-fashioned high comb.
Console. A slim table designed to be used against a wall.
Corner block. A triangular block used in furniture to reinforce joints.
Cornice. A horizontal section on top of a cabinet; it resembles molding.
Crazing. Tiny surface cracks in wood finish often caused by exposure to sun or heat.
Credenza. A small buffet or sideboard.
Crossbanding. A decorative band of veneer inlay with a grain perpendicular to the grain of a furniture piece.
Cyma. An S-shape curve used often in period furniture.
Dado. Paneling or some other decorative treatment fixed on the lower half of a wall; also a grooved cut used in furniture making.
Drawer guide or slide. A plastic, wood, or metal mechanism that controls the position of a drawer as you open or close it.
Drop front. A hinged desk front that conceals drawers and shelves when closed and that opens to become a writing surface.

Dust panel. A thin board between drawers designed to catch shavings from wooden drawer guides. (Furniture with plastic drawer guides doesn't require dust panels.)
Eight-way hand tie. A technique for tying spring coils to a frame; has cords from front to back and side to side and then diagonally across the spring.
Embossed. Any surface with pattern standing out in relief.
Enamel finish. On wood, a coating of enamel paint that's sometimes rubbed to a high gloss. On metal, a baked-on coating.
Étagère. A freestanding open cabinet with shelves for displaying accessories.
Etching. A decorative technique that removes part of top surface to create a design.
Fauteuil. An upholstered armchair with open sides, and usually with upholstered arm or elbow pads.
Fiberfill. Man-made material used as cushioning in upholstered furniture and bedding; it often consists of polyester, acrylic, acetate, or polypropylene fibers.
Fiddle back. A violin-shape splat back on a chair; popular in Queen Anne designs.
Finial. A decorative end on a post or upright.
Float glass. Glass specially processed to give undistorted vision and reflection; used for mirrors.
Gallery. A small railing that borders the top of a table, chest, or cabinet.
Gesso. A mixture of whiting or plaster of paris used as a base for gilding.
Glazed doors. Doors with glass panels, frequently decorated with lattice work.
Grommet. A metal or plastic ring set into a hole in fabric to protect or strengthen the hole.
Hand rub. A wood polishing technique done without machines; felt blocks and pumice or rottenstone are used instead to achieve a deep luster.
Hardwood. Heavy, close-grained wood from broad-leafed or deciduous trees.
Harvest table. A long rectangular table with narrow, hinged drop-leaf sides, usually Colonial in design.
Highboy. A tall chest of four or five drawers on legs, with a cornice or pediment crown.
Hitchcock chair. A small American chair with oval-turned top rail, splayed front legs, and a rush or caned seat; usually black with a painted-on stencil on the back rail.
Hoopback. A chair with a top rail that flows into the arms in one continuous curve; common in Queen Anne and Hepplewhite styles.
H-stretcher. Braces between legs that connect to a center member to form an H shape.
Hutch. An old term for a chest, now used to describe a cupboard; often has open shelves and is set on a cabinet.
Inlay. An ornamentation process in which pieces of wood are excised from the surface, then replaced with pieces of the same shape but of different woods or other materials, such as ivory or mother-of-pearl.
Intaglio. A decorative motif carved or cut below the surface.
Insulator. A sheet of wire-reinforced burlap that separates coils from felt or other filler material in an upholstered piece.
Japanning. A painting technique that imitates Japanese lacquer; separate coats of varnish are hardened with heat.
Kick pleat. An inverted pleat often used at corners of sofa and chair skirts.
Kiln drying. A wood-drying process that uses controlled heat to dry wood evenly. This reduces warping.
Knee. The upper corner of a cabriole leg, commonly carved with a decorative motif.
Knockdown (KD). Furniture shipped from the factory unassembled, to be put together by the customer or retailer.
Lacquer. One of several modern-day finishes that is a mixture of cellulose derivatives and that can be used on wood or metal surfaces.
Ladder-back. A rustic chair with a back that resembles the rungs of a ladder; back posts are joined by a series of horizontal rails.
Laminate. A product made by bonding together layers of wood, plastic, fabric, and paper with heat and pressure.
Linenfold. A decorative treatment, usually carved in wood panels, that resembles folds of linen.
Lowboy. A low chest or table with drawers on high legs, commonly used for serving or as a support for the upper chest of a highboy.
Low relief. Shallow carving.
Lyre. A decorative motif shaped like a harp; popular during the Duncan Phyfe period.
Marlborough leg. A straight, square leg that often ends with a block foot; commonly used by Chippendale.
Marquetry. A decorative pattern made by setting contrasting materials into a veneered surface. Materials such as colored woods, tortoise shell, ivory, and mother-of-pearl were often used to create floral and shell-like patterns.
Moiré. A wavy design on fabric or other material that produces a watery effect.
Nesting tables. Small tables made in sets of graduated sizes so they can stack for easy storage.
Occasional furniture. Small tables, chests, commodes, and pull-up chairs that can be used for varied purposes.
Oil finish. A wood finish achieved with linseed oil or a polish that contains oil.
Ormolu. Ornamentation of gilded brass, copper, or bronze; especially common on seventeenth- and eighteenth-century French pieces.
Ottoman. An upholstered seat without arms or back used as a footstool, or pushed up to a chair to form a chaise.
Oval-back. A chair with an oval-shape back that's either upholstered or open; a popular form for Louis XVI and Hepplewhite chairs.
Pad foot. A flat club foot.
Parsons table. A table designed by Frank A. Parsons of the Parsons School of Design; distinguished by square block legs that form four corners.
Particleboard. Wood panels formed by bonding wood particles together with synthetic resins under heat and pressure; often used for inexpensive furnuture.
Pedestal. A slender column on a furniture base, often carved or fluted.
Pediment. A decorative hood or crown on a cabinet; designs range from angular to gently rounded.
Period furniture. Furnishings that are typical of a particular past historical period, most commonly used in reference to designs from the eighteenth century or earlier.
Pickled finish. Whitened finish that simulates old wood with a chalky residue of paint.

(continued)

A GLOSSARY OF FURNITURE TERMS

(continued)

Pierced work. Ornamental carving in which portions are cut out, leaving a tracery design.
Pier glass. A tall, narrow mirror usually hung above a small console table; originally placed between two windows.
Pilaster. A decorative half column projecting from a piece of furniture; usually fluted or topped with a carved capital.
Plinth. A square, boxlike base for a chair or sofa.
Polypropylene. Tough plastic used to make furniture frames.
Rail. A horizontal element in a chair, sofa, or panel door.
Reproduction. A copy or a close approximation of an original object.
Rolled arm. In upholstery, a padded scroll-like arm that curves up and out from the seat; often tufted or trimmed with welting.
Rolltop desk. A desk equipped with a tambour lid that rolls down to cover the writing surface.
Rosette. A flower-shaped, ornamental design often carved into wood.
Satin finish. A finish with less luster than high gloss.
Scroll foot. A foot with a spiral curl; often used with a cabriole leg.
Scroll top. A broken pediment formed by two cyma curves.
Sealer. A coating used on wood so succeeding coats won't soak into the grain.
Secretary. A tall cabinet with a slant-front desk topped by a bookcase.
Sectional furniture. Upholstery or case pieces made in component units that can be arranged many ways.
Serpentine front. An undulating front surface on a chest of drawers; usually convex in the center and concave on the sides.
Settee. A lightly scaled long seat with arms and a back; a forerunner of today's sofa.
Settle. A high-backed wooden bench with solid front and side panels built to the floor; the seat sometimes is hinged, with storage below.
Shellac. A natural resin used as a prime coat and sealer in wood finishing.
Shield back. A chair back that resembles an open shield; made popular by Hepplewhite.
Sideboard. A serving piece with drawers, open shelves, or both for displaying plates and silver.
Slat-back. A chair with an open back of horizontal cross members; also called ladder-back.
Sling chair. A chair with a seat made by suspending flexible material between side supports.
Slipper chair. A low, armless chair that's often upholstered and trimmed with a long skirt.
Slipper foot. A slender, long club foot; commonly used on Queen Anne furniture.
Softwood. Wood from a coniferous tree.
Spade foot. A square foot that tapers to the base; a popular choice of Hepplewhite.
Splay. The outward slant of a part of furniture; commonly used to describe legs.
Splint seat. A chair seat woven from thin wood strips.
Sponging. A painting technique in which color is applied with a sponge to create a mottled effect; used on some nineteenth-century American country pieces.
Stencil. A decorative motif created by painting through the cut-out spaces of a paper pattern.
Studs. Decorative nailheads often used to trim traditional-style leather furniture.
Suite. A set of matching furniture pieces designed for a particular room, such as a bedroom or dining room.
Swing-leg table. A table with hinged legs that swing out to support drop leaves.
Tambour. A front or sliding cover made of thin wood strips joined and mounted in parallel side grooves; rolltop desks have tambour tops.
T-cushion. A seat cushion shaped like a T; the arms of a chair or sofa fit into the side indentations.
Tea table. A small round or rectangular table with a gallery around its top edge.
Tier table. A small accent table with stacked tops that get smaller as they go up.
Tilt-top table. A small table with a hinged top that can be tilted into a vertical position; originally designed to save space.
Trestle table. A long, narrow table with two T-shaped uprights joined by a single stretcher.
Tub chair. A short lounge chair with a rounded back and tublike profile.
Tufting. In upholstery, a technique used to anchor the cover fabric by sewing it to the filler; decorative tufting often results in tight folds of fabric radiating to a center button.
Turned. A term used to describe a leg or spindle formed on a lathe.
Tuxedo sofa. A modern style of sofa with a square frame and arms that are the same height as the back.
Varnish. Resin that leaves a hard, glossy, transparent coating when applied to wood.
Veneer. A thin slice of fine wood used to resurface less-expensive wood or another material.
Webbing. Linen or jute bands woven to form support for the springs and filler in upholstered furniture; also rubber webbing in some modern furniture, or plastic webbing on outdoor pieces.
Windsor chair. A chair with spindles set into a hoop frame to form the back, a scooped wooden seat, and four splayed legs; introduced in early eighteenth-century England and quickly adapted by American furniture makers.
Wing chair. A high-backed, upholstered easy chair with wings on either side of the chair back; the wings originally kept drafts from chilling the person in the chair.

WHERE TO GO FOR MORE INFORMATION

Better Homes and Gardens® Books
Better Homes and Gardens®
NEW DECORATING BOOK
How to translate ideas into workable solutions for every room in your home. Choosing a style, furniture arrangements, windows, walls and ceilings, floors, lighting, and accessories. 433 color photos, 76 how-to illustrations, 432 pages.

Better Homes and Gardens®
COMPLETE GUIDE TO HOME REPAIR, MAINTENANCE, & IMPROVEMENT
Inside your home, outside your home, your home's systems, basics you should know. Anatomy and step-by-step drawings illustrate components, tools, techniques, and finishes.
515 how-to techniques; 75 charts; 2,734 illustrations; 552 pages.

Other Sources of Information
American Society of Interior Designers (ASID)
730 Fifth Avenue
New York, NY 10019

Carpet Cushion Council
P.O. Box 465
Southfield, MO 48037

Carpet & Rug Institute
P.O. Box 2048
Dalton, GA 30720

Federal Trade Commission, Bureau of Consumer Protection
Washington, DC 20580

Furniture Industry Consumer Advisory Panel (FICAP)
P.O. Box 951
High Point, NC 27261

Man-Made Fiber Producers Association
Suite 310
1150 17th Street NW
Washington, DC 20036

National Association for Bedding Manufacturers (NABM)
1235 Jefferson Davis Highway
Arlington, VA 22202

National Association of Furniture Manufacturers (NAFM)
8401 Connecticut Ave. Suite 911
Washington, DC 20015

Waterbed Manufacturers Association
1411 Olympic Blvd.
Los Angeles, CA 90015

The Wool Bureau, Inc.
360 Lexington Avenue
New York, NY 10017

ACKNOWLEDGMENTS

Architects and Designers
Pages 6-11
Robert E. Dittmer
Pages 14-15
Mel Crum
Pages 16-17
Inez Saunders
Carol Siegmeister
Pages 18-19
Candler Lloyd Interiors, Inc.
Pages 20-21
Robert E. Dittmer
Pages 22-23
Harry & Joyce Niewoehner;
Marilyn Hannigan
Pages 24-25
Robert E. Dittmer
Pages 26-27
Robert & Barbara Thomas;
Nancy Brous, Private Collections
Pages 28-29
Sue Parr
Marvin Ullman
Pages 30-31
Marsha Sewell, ASID;
Eileen Herman, Eileen Herman Custom Interiors
Pages 32-33
Holland & Steed, AIA
Pages 44-45
Carol Knott, ASID
Pages 50-51
Robert E. Dittmer
Pages 52-53
Inter Design, Inc.
Pages 56-57
Jon Cockrell
Pages 64-65
Jesse Benesch & Assoc.
Pages 84-85
Nancy Brous, Private Collections
Page 87
Jay Goldberg;
Joyce Lowenstein, ASID, Townhouse Interiors
Pages 88-89
Robert E. Dittmer
Pages 98-99
Marc Tarasuck;
Barbara Epstein
Pages 100-101
Jeff Hicks;
James Berkon
Pages 102-103
Marsha Sewell, ASID
Pages 104-105
Suzy Taylor;
Joan Coulter
Pages 106-109
Robert E. Dittmer
Pages 110-111
Elayne Becker
Pages 114-117
Dennis Freedman
Page 119
Chet Ross
Page 124
Peggy Walker Interiors
Pages 128-129
Robert Zoller & Kim R. Williamson, ASID
Pages 130-131
David M. Rice, FASID
Pages 132-133
Robert E. Dittmer

Photographers
Jessie Walker
Ross Chapple
William N. Hopkins
Bill Hopkins, Jr.
Maris/Semel
Hedrich-Blessing
Tom Miyasaki
Tim Street-Porter
Scott Little
Mike Dieter
Thomas E. Hopper
George Ceolla
Bradley Olman
Martin Helfer

Special Thanks
Thomasville Furniture Industries, Inc.
The Bartley Collection, Ltd.
Cohasset Colonials
Emperor Clock Co.
Simms & Thayer Cabinetmakers
Van Horn Plastics, Inc.
Workbench
High Point Arts Council
Younkers Store for Homes
Woodstock, Ltd.

INDEX

Page numbers in *italics* refer to photographs or illustrated text.

A-B

C-D

E-K

L-Q

R-S

INDEX

T-Z
